GROUNDWORK
FOR THE METAPHYSICS OF
MORALS

broadview editions
series editor: L.W. Conolly

GROUNDWORK FOR THE METAPHYSICS OF MORALS

Immanuel Kant

translated by Thomas K. Abbott
with revisions by Lara Denis

edited by Lara Denis

broadview editions

Library and Archives Canada Cataloguing in Publication

Kant, Immanuel, 1724–1804.

  Groundwork for the metaphysics of morals / by Immanuel Kant; translated by Thomas K. Abbott; with revisions by Lara Denis; edited by Lara Denis.

(Broadview editions)
Translation of: Grundlegung zur Metaphysik der Sitten.
Includes bibliographical references and index.
ISBN 1-55111-539-5

  1. Ethics—Early works to 1800.   I. Abbott, Thomas Kingsmill, 1829-1913   II. Denis, Lara, 1969-   III. Title.   IV. Series.

B2766.E6D45 2005   170   C2005-900068-6

Broadview Editions

The Broadview Editions series represents the ever-changing canon of literature in English by bringing together texts long regarded as classics with valuable lesser-known works.

Advisory editor for this volume: Kathryn Prince

Broadview Press Ltd. is an independent, international publishing house, incorporated in 1985. Broadview believes in shared ownership, both with its employees and with the general public; since the year 2000 Broadview shares have traded publicly on the Toronto Venture Exchange under the symbol BDP.

We welcome comments and suggestions regarding any aspect of our publications — please feel free to contact us at the addresses below or at broadview@broadviewpress.com.

North America
Post Office Box 1243, Peterborough, Ontario, Canada K9J 7H5
3576 California Road, Orchard Park, NY, USA 14127
Tel: (705) 743-8990; Fax: (705) 743-8353;
email: customerservice@broadviewpress.com

UK, Ireland, and continental Europe
NBN Plymbridge, Estover Road, Plymouth PL6 7PY UK
Tel: 44 (0) 1752 202301   Fax: 44 (0) 1752 202331
Fax Order Line: 44 (0) 1752 202333
Customer Service: cservs@nbnplymbridge.com   Orders: orders@nbnplymbridge.com

Australia and New Zealand
UNIREPS, University of New South Wales
Australia Sydney, NSW, 2052
Tel: 61 2 9664 0999; Fax: 61 2 9664 5420
email: info.press@unsw.edu.au

www.broadviewpress.com

Typesetting and assembly: True to Type Inc., Mississauga, Canada.

PRINTED IN CANADA

For Emmanuel Tseklenis Denis
and Lorraine Williams Denis

Contents

Acknowledgements

I would like to thank Don LePan for encouraging me to submit a proposal for Kant's *Groundwork* to Broadview, Julia Gaunce for assisting me during the proposal process, and the anonymous referees for helping me refine my proposal. Thanks to Bill Bristow for helping me decide what should be included in the appendices, to Rebecca Yurman for proofreading a partial draft of the manuscript, and to Frederick Raucher for commenting on the entire manuscript. Thanks also to Barbara M. Conolly, Leonard Conolly, Kathryn Prince, Tania Therien, and everyone else at Broadview who helped turn the manuscript into this book. Finally, thanks to my husband, Roger Wertheimer, for commenting on a draft of the introduction, and (more importantly) for being a constant source of love and support, as well as a frequent source of perplexity and amusement.

Introduction

Immanuel Kant's *Groundwork for the Metaphysics of Morals* (1785) is one of the most read and least understood works of Western philosophy.

The *Groundwork* is widely read because it is the foundational ethical work of one of the most important, influential philosophers. Kant's notions of autonomy, morality as a categorical imperative, and the dignity of rational nature, all found in the *Groundwork*, have had a profound influence on moral and political philosophy from his time forward. Kant himself wrote many books and essays on moral and political philosophy, as well as works in metaphysics, epistemology, logic, philosophy of religion, aesthetics, and other areas. Kant was the most significant philosopher of the Enlightenment, a period famous for its optimism regarding the power of human rationality. His work heavily influenced philosophers from his own time forward—from German and British idealists such as G.W.F. Hegel and F.H. Bradley to contemporary liberal theorists such as John Rawls and Robert Nozick.[1] Additionally, the *Groundwork*'s brevity makes it appear accessible.

The *Groundwork* is widely misunderstood because it is often read in isolation from Kant's other works of moral philosophy. As a result, this one important part of his ethical theory is mistaken for the whole. This work with very specific, theoretically abstract goals has been expected to provide, and has been interpreted as though it provides, a complete moral theory. Claims and arguments specific to the project of the *Groundwork* are read as though they offer normative guidance (i.e., guidance about what to do) that Kant never intended them to give. Of course, some misunderstandings of the *Groundwork* are due to Kant's style: often technical, terse, and convoluted in turn.

This edition aims to reduce the barriers to understanding and appreciating Kant's *Groundwork*. The introduction and editorial notes in the text provide assistance with Kant's terms, arguments, and claims. This introduction neither fully reconstructs Kant's

---

1   Kant-influenced works of these philosophers include Hegel's *Philosophy of Right*, trans. E.S. Haldane and Frances H. Simson (New York: Humanities Press, 1955 [1892]), Bradley's *Ethical Studies* (Oxford: Clarendon, 1876), Rawls's *A Theory of Justice* (Cambridge, MA: Belknap Press of Harvard University, 1971), and Nozick's *Anarchy, State, and Utopia* (New York: Basic Books, 1974).

arguments nor interprets Kant in great depth; these are the essential tasks for the reader—or, if the reader is a student, for the reader together with his or her classmates and professor. Rather, this introduction sets out Kant's goals and strategies in the *Groundwork* as a whole and in each of its sections, sketches some of its main arguments, and highlights issues of interpretive and philosophical debate. Notes in the introduction point the reader to books and articles that offer interpretations and evaluations of *Groundwork* arguments.

More fundamentally, this edition aims to facilitate a fair, rich understanding of the *Groundwork* by placing it in the context of Kant's other works, as well as in the context of criticisms of the *Groundwork* and of Kant's ethics more broadly. This context is furnished by the appendices, and the notes in the text which allude to them. The appendices include portions of Kant's other ethical writings, the *Critique of Practical Reason* (1788) and the *Metaphysics of Morals* (both the "Doctrine of Right" and the "Doctrine of Virtue") (1797); ethically relevant portions of *Religion within the Limits of Reason Alone* and "On the Common Saying: 'This May Be True in Theory, but It Does Not Apply in Practice'" (both 1793); all of "What is Enlightenment?" (1784); and criticisms of Kant's ethics by Friedrich von Schiller in *Xenian* (1796), J.G. Fichte in a letter to Reinhold (1795), G.W.F. Hegel in *Lectures on the History of Philosophy* (1831), and Henry Sidgwick in *The Methods of Ethics* (1907). The portions of Kant's works appended have been chosen to give the reader a fuller sense of Kant's ethical theory as a whole, the better to appreciate the place of the *Groundwork* within it. The appended criticisms reveal how Kant's ethics, especially his *Groundwork*, has been received by other influential philosophers, beginning with his contemporaries. The criticisms expressed in these appendices have themselves been influential. No doubt readers will see some of their own objections or questions expressed in them. Readers are encouraged to look not only to the *Groundwork*, but also to the appended portions of Kant's other works, when considering how Kant might respond to these objections.

Background[1]

Immanuel Kant (1724-1804) was born in Königsberg, Prussia to Johann Georg Kant (1683-1746), a harness maker, and Anna

---

1 Much of this information is drawn from Manfred Kuehn, *Kant: A Biography* (Cambridge: Cambridge UP, 2001).

Regina Kant (1697-1737). Four of Kant's eight siblings died in childhood. Kant's mother died when he was only thirteen.

Kant's family were Pietists, evangelical Protestants who focused on morality, charity, and a personal relationship to God, and rejected the elaborate ceremony and highly intellectual theological dogma of orthodox Protestantism. Kant attended the Pietist *Collegium Fridericianum* as a day student from age eight to sixteen, though he hated the stern discipline and religious fanaticism he found there. Kant did not participate in organized religion as an adult. Elements of both Pietism and anti-Pietism can be seen in Kant's philosophy of religion.

The education Kant received at the *Collegium Fridericianum* provided him with a solid foundation in classical languages and literatures. Kant went on to the University of Königsberg, where he studied philosophy, history, mathematics, and physics. From 1748-55, before Kant became a lecturer, financial need led him to work as a tutor in private homes. In this capacity, which he found generally unpleasant, Kant formed some of his views not only about child-rearing and education, but also about social inequality.

As a lecturer at the University of Königsberg, Kant's range of topics was vast, encompassing theology, logic, mathematics, physics, metaphysics, physical geography, ethics, and anthropology. Kant became a professor in 1770, at which point he was able to devote less time to lecturing and more to writing. The range of Kant's written work is as expansive as that of his lectures. Kant's best known works include the *Critique of Pure Reason* (1781, 1787) and *Prolegomena to any Future Metaphysics* (1783), in metaphysics and epistemology; *Groundwork for the Metaphysics of Morals, Critique of Practical Reason*, and *Metaphysics of Morals* in ethics; the *Critique of the Power of Judgment* (1790) in aesthetics; and *Religion within the Limits of Reason Alone* in philosophy of religion. Kant wrote numerous influential essays as well, including "Toward Perpetual Peace" (1795) and "Conjectures on the Beginning of Human History" (1786). Notes from Kant's lectures on such topics as anthropology, education, ethics, logic, and philosophical theology were also published, most after his death.

Among the early influences on Kant were Isaac Newton's (1642-1727) physics and the Leibniz-Wolff school of metaphysics and epistemology. As a lecturer, Kant often referred to Jean-Jacques Rousseau's (1712-78) views on education, human nature, and equality. Kant's early views about morality were influenced by, among other approaches, Christian Wolff's (1679-1754) rational-ism and perfectionism and Francis Hutcheson's (1694-1746) sentimentalism. David Hume (1711-76) influenced Kant's thoughts both in ethics and in metaphysics and epistemology. Moses Mendelssohn (1729-86) was a valued philosophical correspondent. Schiller and Christian Garve (1742-98) were critics Kant sought to answer. Johann Gottfried von Herder (1744-1803) was a student who went on to develop a strong influence in German philosophy in his own right, rejecting many of Kant's own views. Fichte enjoyed early support from Kant, but soon turned critical of Kant's philosophy and lost Kant's favor.

Although Kant's written work, notably the *Critique of Pure Reason* and the *Groundwork*, attracted much scholarly controversy, it was *Religion within the Limits of Reason Alone* that attracted unwanted political attention. The trouble began in 1788, two years after Frederick William II replaced the deceased Frederick the Great as King of Prussia. The Spiritual Affairs Commission issued edicts demanding that professors in public universities (and others in the public employ) adhere to Protestant orthodoxy in their lectures and writings. In 1794, the king signed a Cabinet Order which forbade Kant to profess publicly his views on religion. Kant promised to comply with the edict, but he took his promise as one to the king only, and so saw himself as free to resume lecturing and publishing on religion after Frederick William II's death in 1797.

Kant lived his entire life in Königsberg and its vicinity; he never traveled. He relished hearing about other countries, cultures, and customs from those who did travel, however. Kant never married, but his social life was active nonetheless. He was known to enjoy dinner parties, and he had many friends, including philosophers, other academics, business people, politicians, and former students.

Groundwork for the Metaphysics of Morals

Overview

The tasks Kant sets for himself in the *Groundwork* are "the investigation and establishment of *the supreme principle of morality*" (G 4:392),[1] from which all other moral principles, duties, and

---

1   Page references throughout the introduction are to the Prussian Academy edition of Kant's complete works (including volume numbers—or, in the case of the *Critique of Pure Reason*, "A" and "B," indicating first and

rights ultimately follow. Kant does not take this project to involve inventing a new moral principle. Rather, Kant sees his mission as that of rendering explicit and free of extraneous, misleading associations, a principle already fundamental and implicit in moral thought (G 4:403-404).

Kant explains the nature and necessity of his project in the Preface. In Sections 1 and 2, he draws on some of our most basic notions of morality to articulate criteria for a supreme moral principle. Beginning near the end of Section 1, and continuing through Section 2, Kant presents several versions of what he takes to be a single principle that meets these criteria, arguing that *if there is a supreme moral principle*, this principle (which he calls *"the categorical imperative"* [CI]) *is it.*[1] Thus, Sections 1 and 2 take care of much of the *investigation* of the supreme moral principle. But note that Kant's conclusion up to this point is conditional: he stops short of claiming that we are *in fact* bound by this principle—or any moral principle whatever—leaving the crucial task of the supreme moral principle's *establishment* for Section 3.

Kant describes his overall approach in Sections 1 and 2 as "analytical" because his arguments proceed largely by analyzing accepted claims about such things as moral requirement and moral motivation to see what they presuppose. Kant calls his style of argument in Section 3 "synthetic" both because he constructively defends the propositions and concepts he derived analytically in Sections 1 and 2 so that they can in turn be used to defend the claims from which they were derived, and because the main argument of the third section—the argument for the bindingness of the categorical imperative for us—involves *connecting* the independent concepts of rational nature and the supreme moral principle to one another by means of a third term, membership in the "intelligible world," which our freedom reveals to us.

---

second editions), prefaced by an abbreviation identifying the work in which it can be found: CJ = *Critique of the Power of Judgment*, trans. Werner S. Pluhar (Indianapolis: Hackett, 1987); CprR = *Critique of Practical Reason*; CpuR = *Critique of Pure Reason*; G = *Groundwork for the Metaphysics of Morals*, this translation; E = *Education*; MM = *Metaphysics of Morals*, trans. Mary J. Gregor (Cambridge: Cambridge UP, 1996); Rel = *Religion within the Limits of Reason Alone*, trans. Allen Wood and George di Giovanni (Cambridge: Cambridge UP, 1998). Citations in bold refer to material in the appendices of this edition.

1 This argument is the subject of Samuel J. Kerstein, *Kant's Search for the Supreme Principle of Morality* (Cambridge: Cambridge UP, 2002).

Kant's Preface

Kant's Preface aims to locate ethics in relation to other branches of philosophy, distinguish different parts of moral philosophy, and explain the rationale for the *Groundwork*. I will say a few words about the latter goals.

Kant distinguishes between rational or "pure" moral philosophy and empirical moral philosophy, which he also calls "anthropology." Empirical moral philosophy concerns how people act; it is based on *a posteriori* principles, those derived from observation and experience. Pure moral philosophy, by contrast, concerns how people ought to act; it is based on *a priori* principles, those inherent in and revealed by the operations of reason (G 4:389). Pure moral philosophy is the subject of the *Groundwork*.

In the Preface as well as later in the *Groundwork*, Kant stresses the importance of not mixing empirical and pure parts of moral philosophy (G 4:388-93, 410). One of his reasons for this caution is that doing so could lead us to fasten not onto the true supreme moral principle, but onto some other, less authoritative principle. Kant takes our notion of moral requirement to presuppose a principle valid for all rational beings—i.e., beings who can rationally reflect on and decide what to do. Kant thinks we take all the moral duties we have as human beings to be grounded in some more general principle that holds for all rational beings of any species. If we were not careful to keep clear of empirical moral philosophy when trying to locate the supreme principle of morality, Kant thinks, we might accidently end up basing our alleged supreme moral principle on observations about how human beings actually act, or about what things are good for beings of our particular species. In short, we would come up with an empirical generalization, or some prudential guides helpful to human beings, but not with a supreme moral principle (G 4:389-90).

Kant also argues that the supreme moral principle must be sought out and established prior to constructing an account of the moral duties humans have to themselves and one another, which is what Kant does in the *Metaphysics of Morals*, and prior to considering how to conduct ourselves and interact with others so as to facilitate the fulfillment of these duties, something Kant discusses in his *Anthropology from a Pragmatic Point of View* (1798). Thus, the purpose of the *Groundwork* is to provide the pure, rational foundation for the rest of Kant's moral theory. Indeed, one of his claims in the Preface is that there has yet to be such a pure foundation for moral theory articulated.

Given Kant's stated intention of separating pure moral philosophy from empirical, and focusing exclusively on pure moral philosophy in the *Groundwork*, readers are sometimes confused by Kant's references to particular duties or examples from human life (e.g., G 4:399). Kant does indeed draw on common assumptions about human nature and morality at various stages of his arguments in the *Groundwork*. Most commentators do not think Kant undermines his project by using these assumptions and examples, as long as he employs them in order to, say, reveal aspects of our *a priori* concept of morality, or to show that a candidate moral principle illuminates the logic behind widely accepted judgments. But the reader is encouraged to look at when and how Kant does draw on examples of human conduct, or on judgments about particular duties, and to think about why he does so, and whether he does so within his self-chosen parameters.

It is also worth noting that many ethicists reject Kant's view of and approach to ethics. Virtue ethicists, such as Aristotle and his contemporary followers, think that ethics is the study of how to live well as a human being.[1] There may well be some universal principles according to this approach, but the scope of universality will be human beings, not rational beings—even though, for Aristotle, our rationality is an essential and important aspect of our human nature, and greatly shapes his account of how we can flourish as human beings. Though Kant's ethics has some important things in common with Aristotle's, Kant takes Aristotle's notion of what ethics is about to be misguided. Again, for Kant, focusing on human beings as such, rather than focusing first on rational beings generally, and then later on human beings as one category of rational beings, prevents us from locating the supreme principle of morality. It locks us into a lower level of analysis, the result of which cannot be a morally authoritative principle.

Section One

Section 1 of the *Groundwork* aims to take us from the idea of a "good will" to a rough formulation of the supreme moral principle, a formulation similar to what Kant will call the "formula of

---

1 See Aristotle, *Nicomachean Ethics*, second edition, trans. Terence Irwin (Indianapolis: Hackett, 1999). Among contemporary Aristotelian virtue ethicists are John McDowell, author of "Virtue and Reason," *The Monist* 62 (1979): 331-50 (reprinted in *Virtue Ethics*, ed. Roger Crisp and Michael Slote [New York: Oxford UP, 1997]); and Rosalind Hursthouse, author of *On Virtue Ethics* (New York: Oxford UP, 1999).

universal law" in Section 2. Kant begins with what he views as the shared presumption that a good will—that is, the commitment to do one's duty simply because it is right—has a special kind of value, and analyzes the notion of a good will in order to ascertain the principle on which a good will acts (insofar as it is good). In identifying the principle which exemplifies the willing of a good will, Kant believes, we identify the supreme moral principle.[1] Kant then goes on to illustrate this principle through examples, contrast it with principles of prudential reasoning, and reiterate the philosophical and practical importance of pursuing pure moral philosophy prior to and independently of empirical moral philosophy.

Kant's main argument proceeds roughly as follows. The good will is the only thing in the world that is good unconditionally and in itself, no matter what it accomplishes, or what other attributes (such as wealth or skill) accompany it. Only actions done from duty have "moral worth," that is, reflect the intrinsic, unconditional value of a good will. We can discover the principle of a good will (and thus the supreme moral principle) by analyzing the nature of actions done from duty. The moral worth of actions done from duty comes just from the ground, or fundamental maxim (subjective practical principle),[2] of the actions, not from the purposes ("ends") the agent aims at through those actions (e.g., one's own survival or the happiness of others). Action done from duty has a formal (reason-based) principle, not a material (inclination-based) principle as its ground; for the good will chooses to promote inclination-based ends only if they are compatible with or required by morality, and thus the promotion of such ends cannot itself constitute the fundamental, constitutive principle of such a will. (So though a principle of maximizing happiness is not ruled out as a subsidiary moral principle, such a Utilitarian principle could not, according to this line of argument, be the supreme moral principle.)[3] Action done from duty is action

---

1 Christine M. Korsgaard provides a reconstruction of Kant's "motivational analysis" in "Kant's Analysis of Obligation: The Argument of *Groundwork I*" in *Creating the Kingdom of Ends* (Cambridge: Cambridge UP, 1996).

2 Maxims will be explained below, in the context of the formula of universal law (FUL).

3 R.M. Hare argues that one reaches a certain kind of Utilitarianism as one's normative moral theory if one accepts Kant's views about the "universal prescriptivity" of moral judgment. See, e.g., *Moral Thinking: Its Levels, Method and Point* (New York: Oxford UP, 1981).

done from respect for the law. This respect is reflected in the form of the maxims constitutive of a good will: their form is compatible with universal, practical law. So the principle of a good will and thus (one articulation of) the supreme moral principle is: "I am never to act otherwise than so that I could at the same time will that my maxim should be a universal law" (G 4:402).

There are certainly a number of points at which one could raise questions or objections to Kant's argument of Section 1. One of the earliest, best-known, and most frequently voiced objections to Kant's *Groundwork* pertains to Kant's claims that what is special about a good will is that it "acts from duty" rather than from inclination or impulse, and this purity of motive gives acts "moral worth." Many commentators have objected that acting from duty (at best) provides too narrow an account of morally worthy acts or (at worst) is repugnant. Some commentators have even worried that Kant's view of the moral worth of acting from duty implies that it is desirable to lack sympathy and love for others so that one can achieve moral worth of helping them from duty and contrary to inclination![1]

I will discuss a few replies to this objection. First, one can act from duty without acting against one's inclinations. Indeed, one can act from duty even when one's inclinations agree with duty. One acts from duty when what motivates one to act is the rightness of the act; when one does the right thing for the reason that makes it right. According to Kant, nothing is ever right simply because one has an impulse to do it, or because it would satisfy one's sympathetic feelings to do it. Thus, action fundamentally motivated by an inclination or feeling could not reflect the sort of commitment to morality emblematic of a good will. And since what it is for an act to have moral worth is for it to reflect the goodness distinctive of the good will's commitment to morality, no act motivated fundamentally by an impulse, inclination, or feeling can have moral worth.[2]

---

1   See Appendix G for Schiller's version of this objection, and Appendix C for Kant's attempt to clarify the nature of moral motivation in "On the Common Saying: 'This May Be True in Theory, but It Does Not Apply in Practice.'"

2   Among the illuminating explorations of this issue are Barbara Herman, "On the Value of Acting from the Motive of Duty" in *The Practice of Moral Judgment* (Cambridge, MA: Harvard UP, 1993) and chapter 4 of Marcia Baron, *Kantian Ethics Almost without Apology* (Ithaca, NY: Cornell UP, 1995).

Second, moral worth is a specific kind of moral value. Just because acts motivated by sympathy or self-interest cannot have moral worth, that does not mean that they lack moral value altogether. Kant explicitly says that certain feelings and inclinations are morally valuable in other (albeit less fundamental) ways, such as by facilitating the effectiveness of a good will, or by motivating people to act rightly even when they are not motivated by duty. Kant says that "moderation in the affections and passions, self-control, and calm deliberation are ... good in many respects" (G 4:394) as are "courage, resolution, [and] perseverance" (G 4:393); and he says that "the inclination to honor ... deserves praise and encouragement" in so far as it accords with duty (G 4:398). Moral worth is the special kind of moral value that Kant thinks we attribute to acts that express the agent's commitment to morality—something acts motivated by inclination instead of duty cannot do, even when these acts are morally permissible and even if the agent would have refrained from doing them if they were wrong.

Third, Kant's notion of the good will is not tantamount to his notion of a virtuous human agent. We must keep in mind Kant's project at this stage of the *Groundwork*, and in the *Groundwork* as a whole. This is not a work of normative ethics, in which Kant tells us what our duties are, and what sorts of people we should try to be. Kant's aim is to investigate and establish the supreme principle of morality. In Section 1, he is trying to do this by analyzing the notion of a good will. To elucidate the good will's nature, to clarify how it chooses what to do so as to discern its principle, Kant needs to distinguish what's special about the good will's willing from other ways one might choose what to do. So Kant's examples of a bitter, sad person helping not from love but from duty (G 4:398-99), and of a depressed person going on with life not out of self-love but out of duty (G 4:397-98), are not there to serve as examples of the kind of people we should aspire to be like. They are there to highlight the motive of duty, and they do so specifically by removing the other incentives for helping others or going on with life that most mentally healthy, morally committed people have. When Kant talks about virtue, he makes it clear that we should cultivate the disposition to help others.[1]

---

1 See **MM 443, 457** in Appendix E.

Section Two

In Section 2, Kant articulates his notion of the supreme principle of morality as a categorical imperative, presents several versions of the categorical imperative, and explains his notion of autonomy.

According to Kant, moral agents are rational beings, beings who can act on principle, who can reflect on their options and choose what to do. Perfectly rational agents (those with "holy" wills) always do what their reason determines to be good, effortlessly following principles of reason (G 4:412-14). Beings who are not perfectly rational, however, sometimes choose to act in ways contrary to reason. For these imperfectly rational beings, rational principles present them with commands, which Kant calls imperatives (G 4:413). Humans are among the imperfect rational beings who experience rational principles as imperatives; we are obligated by reason to follow these principles, even though perfectly rational beings follow them without any such constraint.

Hypothetical imperatives command agents to take necessary, available means to the ends they have adopted (G 4:414). Hypothetical imperatives are contingent. They bind agents only on the condition that the agents have chosen to pursue some end. Agents can release themselves from most hypothetical imperatives simply by abandoning the end in question. For example, if your end is becoming a lawyer, and a necessary means to that end that is in your power is attending law school, you are rationally required to attend law school. But you are free to abandon this goal of becoming a lawyer; and if you do so, you will be released from the requirement to go to law school. That hypothetical imperative will no longer be binding on you, though it still expresses the valid principle that going to law school is a necessary means to becoming a lawyer.

Kant takes the end of one's own happiness to be one that all finite rational beings with needs do have and cannot rationally abandon, given their nature as rational human beings (G 4:415-19). Imperatives pertaining to the achievement of happiness are still hypothetical, however. An imperative of prudence would not say that an act was good in itself, but that it was good as a means to a further end, happiness (G 4:416). Moreover, because of the vague, fluctuating, and empirical nature of happiness, happiness is not a sufficiently determinate end to generate determinate imperatives. Happiness is a "meta" end, composed of all the other inclination-based ends agents choose. Different people's conceptions of happiness differ depending on their specific ends. The same person's conception of happiness differs over time, as ends are adopted, abandoned, or reordered in priority. Furthermore, the general concept of happiness is that of maximal present and future well-being, yet we lack the foresight ever to know which courses of action would lead to happiness (G 4:418-19). Kant suggests it might be better to think not of "imperatives" of prudence, but "counsels" of prudence, which recommend (for example) that we develop traits such as frugality that tend to benefit most people, regardless of their more specific ends (G 4:418).

Morality, however, presents us not with hypothetical imperatives, but a categorical one. It expresses the necessity of acting in accordance with the supreme principle of morality, no matter what we want to do, or what we are like. One cannot "opt out" of moral requirements. Compliance with the principle of morality is necessary for all rational beings, regardless of what ends they adopt independently of that requirement, and thus is unconditional. For beings who lack holy wills, then, the supreme principle of morality amounts to a categorical imperative. Kant seems to assume that there can be only one categorical imperative: this imperative is the ultimate authority about what we may and may not do, so cannot have a rival.

Kant derives the first formulation of the categorical imperative, the formula of universal law (FUL), from the very idea of a categorical imperative as commanding simply that one's maxims conform to the idea of universal law: "Act only on that maxim whereby you can at the same time will that it become a universal law" (G 4:421). He then introduces a variant, the formula of the universal law of nature (FULN): "Act as if the maxim of your action were to become by your will a universal law of nature" (G 4:421). A maxim is a principle of an agent's will. According to Kant, all actions that can be attributed to us as agents (so, e.g., not metabolizing food, sneezing, or passing out) have maxims underlying them, even though we are not always conscious of them, and can even deceive ourselves about what they are. Maxims of actions contain (at minimum) an agent's conception of an end (whether a purpose to bring about, or an ideal to approximate, or something else) and an act, which is the agent's proposed means to that end. Someone's maxims of actions might include, "I will run every morning in order to get fit" or "I will stand for the pledge of allegiance in order to honor my country." Agents also have higher-level, more long-term maxims, which specify the ends they seek to promote, maintain, honor, and so on, without specifying means to those ends; an example of such a "maxim of ends" is "I will pursue social justice." In his exposition and illustration of FUL and FULN (FUL/N), Kant implies that we can understand some maxims of actions commonly viewed as wrong (contrary to "perfect" duties to oneself and to others) as maxims that cannot consistently be *conceived* as universal laws of nature. Kant argues that we can understand the requirement to adopt certain maxims of ends (e.g., "I will promote the happiness of others") in terms of the impossibility of *willing* maxims of refusing to promote these ends (G 4:424). Kant calls the requirements to promote such ends "imperfect" duties. There is much flexibility regarding how to promote the ends in question, and particular acts of promoting those ends are rarely strictly required.[1]

There has been much debate over how to understand the application of FUL/N to the four cases Kant presents, what the universalizability "tests" are supposed to accomplish, how they are supposed to work, and whether they work. Commentators have often taken FUL/N as a decision procedure through which we can test maxims and determine which maxims are forbidden, necessary, or permissible. That is, they have taken Kant to be claiming that we can take a maxim, ask, "can it be willed at the same time as a universal law (of nature)?" and depending on the answer know whether the maxim is morally required (the maxim of the act or end can be universalized, but the maxim of rejecting the act or end cannot), permissible (the maxim and its contrary are universalizable), or forbidden (the maxim cannot be universalized, but the maxim of rejecting the act or end in question can be). Commentators have also frequently objected that FUL/N fails in this capacity, because it generates false negatives or false positives. That is, FUL/N indicates that clearly permissible maxims fail the universalizability test and so are wrong (false negatives), or that obviously impermissible maxims pass the test and so are right (false positives). A maxim of always buying baseball cards but never selling any cannot be willed at the same time as a universal law, but seems permissible nonetheless, whereas a maxim of

---

1 Ultimately, Kant thinks we can trace agents' maxims back to a supreme commitment, either to the moral law, or to self-love. See Part 1 of *Religion within the Limits of Reason Alone*, including **Rel 6:36**.

killing a noisy neighbor so that one can get some sleep does seem universalizable, despite being obviously and seriously wrong.[1]

There are a number of ways one may try to defend Kant from objections to FUL/N. One approach is to grant that FUL/N is supposed to serve as a decision procedure, but to explain that there are a number of requirements on how we formulate the maxim to be tested. Most obviously, it must be a true, accurate description of the maxim as it is constructed by (and seems choice-worthy to) the agent; it cannot be a trumped-up rationale for the act in question, designed so as to pass the FUL/N test. Moreover, some have argued that the maxims to be tested have to be at a certain level of generality—e.g., neither including details like persons' names or days of the week, nor staying so general that anything from killing kittens to knitting could be understood to fall under the maxim in question. Indeed, this concern about the level of specificity is often linked to the importance of capturing why the agent really desires to perform the act in the first place.[2]

Another approach is to focus on the various kinds of universalization Kant draws on in his examples in the hope that one or more of these, properly understood (and in conjunction with the proper level of maxim specification), will allow FUL/N to work as a decision procedure. Kant's suicide example seems to work with a *teleological* notion of universal laws, in which the problem with the suicide maxim in question is that the natural end of self-love would be frustrated (G 4:421-22). His false promising example seems to work with a *practical* interpretation of universalization, such that the maxim fails because the agent willing it could not succeed in using it to get what she seeks if everyone else acted on that same maxim (G 4:422). Finally, Kant describes FUL/N in connection with perfect duties as revealing a contradiction in conception, which takes the problem with the maxim and its universalization to be one of *logical* contradiction: one cannot consistently conceive a world in which both everyone makes false

---

1 On the issue of FUL/N and violence, see Barbara Herman, "Murder and Mayhem" in *The Practice of Moral Judgment* (Cambridge, MA: Harvard UP, 1993). See Appendices F and H for Fichte's and Hegel's objections to FUL/N.

2 See Onora O'Neill, "Universal Laws and Ends-in-Themselves" in *Constructions of Reason: Explorations of Kant's Practical Philosophy* (Cambridge: Cambridge UP, 1989), and Onora Nell (O'Neill), *Acting on Principle: An Essay on Kantian Ethics* (New York: Columbia UP, 1975).

promises and the institution of promising exists (G 4:424). These are three distinct notions of contradiction, and one might try to argue that some work better than others, or that all are appropriate and work in combination.[1]

A third approach is to argue that, contrary to how many commentators interpret Kant's aims in section 2, FUL/N is not supposed to work alone, on individual maxims, to decide the permissibility of given acts. Perhaps certain background assumptions are necessary, e.g., to show why maxims of killing cannot be willed as universal law.[2] Even if FUL/N can sometimes help us figure out what our duties are, perhaps it must do so by drawing on elements of later versions of the categorical imperative, such as the more intuitive formula of humanity, which tells us always to act in ways that show respect for rational nature, or the formula of the kingdom of ends, which asks us to think in terms of a harmonious system of persons and their maxims.

Finally, one might defend Kant by denying that FUL/N is supposed to serve as a decision procedure at all.[3] According to this line of thought, Kant uses the four examples simply to illustrate that gauging the consistency of one's maxims with the universalized version of the maxim is latent in our moral thinking. It is a long way to go from that to the claim that any particular universalization test is necessary or sufficient to reveal all our moral duties. Indeed, when Kant details and explains our duties in the *Metaphysics of Morals*, he rarely appeals to the formula of universal law. More often, he uses the formula of humanity, or the "supreme principle of the doctrine of virtue," which combines terminology of universalization with terminology of respect for rational nature, emphasizing the latter (**MM 6:395**).

Each of these responses has some plausibility and textual support, though none is without difficulties. Moreover, they all illuminate aspects of Kant's moral thinking and call attention to places where further clarification is needed. The reader is urged to

---

1 Christine M. Korsgaard distinguishes among these interpretations, favoring the practical, in "Kant's Formula of Universal Law" in *Creating the Kingdom of Ends* (New York: Cambridge UP, 1996).

2 See, again, Korsgaard, "Kant's Formula of Universal Law."

3 See, for example, Barbara Herman, "Leaving Deontology Behind" in *The Practice of Moral Judgment*; Chapter 3 of Allen W. Wood, *Kant's Ethical Thought* (Cambridge: Cambridge UP, 1999); and "What is Kantian Ethics?" in Immanuel Kant, *Groundwork for the Metaphysics of Morals*, ed. and trans. Allen W. Wood (New Haven, CT: Yale UP, 2002).

learn from each response and think about how it makes sense to specify maxims for moral examination; what kind of universalization Kant seems to have in mind; whether it is all right for him to draw on more than one kind; how much FUL/N is or should be expected to do on its own, apart from other formulations of the categorical imperative; and whether, given the tasks and methods of the *Groundwork* (and the *Metaphysics of Morals*) it makes sense to treat FUL/N as a decision procedure at all.

After his discussion of FUL/N, Kant presents a formulation of the categorical imperative, the formula of humanity (FH), that may seem surprising in light of his previous claims that the supreme moral principle is formal and not material. FH says: "So act as to treat humanity, whether in your own person or in that of any other, in every case at the same time as an end, never as a means only" (G 4:429). "Humanity," or "rational nature," is the capacity to set, organize, and pursue ends. In calling rational nature an end, Kant is not saying it is a state of affairs to be brought about. Kant calls rational nature an "independently existing end" to be "considered only negatively" (G 4:437). By this he means that it is something that already exists and that is to be respected, sustained, and fostered. Nor does Kant's calling rational nature an end imply that FH is a "material principle," ineligible to be a categorical imperative. In arguing that the supreme moral principle must be formal rather than material, Kant's point was that it could not be grounded in an end chosen on the basis of inclination—a "contingent" end that one may adopt or reject, "relative" to one's species' needs or individual preferences. According to Kant, however, rational nature is not an inclination-based end but an "objective" end, "necessary" for all rational beings.[1] Indeed, Kant suggests that understanding the categorical imperative as containing an end is crucial for understanding how the categorical imperative is "connected (completely *a priori*) with the very concept of a rational being as such" (G 4:426), something he takes to be one of the criteria that the candidate for the supreme moral principle must meet. Identifying an end of the CI is supposed to substantiate this connection because rational beings as such will by reference to ends: if the CI is valid for rational beings as such, the CI should be conceivable as directing the

---

1 For a helpful discussion of FH, see chapter 4 of Allen W. Wood, *Kant's Ethical Thought*.

willing of rational beings by reference to a supremely valuable, rationally necessary end, "an end in itself."

Precisely how Kant argues for FH, and whether this argument is valid and convincing, is one of the important interpretive issues stemming from this part of Section 2. Kant seems to give three (perhaps interdependent) arguments for FH. One says that if we assume there is an end inherent in the CI, rational nature must be that end: no other candidate, such as ends based on inclinations, or inclinations themselves, is valued as an end in itself; only rational nature seems plausibly understood that way (G 4:428). A second, more difficult to interpret, argument can be understood to say that in her capacity as an agent, every rational being implicitly and necessarily regards her rational nature as having a value above that of any of her discretionary ends, which other rational beings should recognize, and thus is rationally required to attribute that same value to other rational beings, and to act in ways consonant with the value of her own and others' rational nature (G 4:429).[1] A third argument says that rational nature is the only end that can be understood as the end of a good will, insofar as we understand that will as unconditionally good. For Kant, understanding a good will as unconditionally good implies understanding it apart from any external end which it aims to bring about. Yet rational nature is not an end that one must bring about. Moreover, rational nature is inherent in, and essential to, a good will, not external to it. Thus, a good will's having rational nature as its end does not involve a good will's subordinating itself to any other object, but rather involves its endorsing its own continuing possibility (G 4:437).

FH, the command to treat rational nature in oneself and others as an end and not as a means only, amounts to a requirement always to treat the capacity to set, organize, and pursue ends as valuable independently of, and as more valuable than, any of the ends a rational being chooses with that capacity. The general requirement to respect rational nature gives rise to more specific moral requirements, some types of which are illustrated by Kant's four examples: duties to oneself (examples 1 and 3) require respect for one's own rational nature; duties to others (examples 2 and 4) require respect for the rational nature of others; perfect

---

1 Part of the difficulty with this argument is that it relies on a premise, about the standpoint we take up as agents, that Kant does not establish until Section 3.

duties (examples 1 and 2) require us to reject maxims of actions showing a willingness to impair, manipulate, or otherwise degrade rational nature; and imperfect duties (examples 3 and 4) require us to foster, support, advance or otherwise honor rational nature. Kant's use of the four examples to illustrate FH is generally regarded as more successful than his use of them to illustrate FUL/N. The perfect duty to oneself to reject maxims of suicide to avoid pain (example 1) can be understood as grounded in the requirement not to treat one's rational nature as less valuable than a merely desired end (the prevention of suffering) (G 4:429). The perfect duty to others not to make a false promise (example 2) can be understood as grounded in the requirement not to treat another person's rational capacities as though their value lay simply in being a tool for one's achievement of one's ends (in this case, by manipulating that rational nature) (G 4:429-30). The imperfect duty to develop one's talents (example 3) can be understood as grounded in the requirement to treat one's rational nature as deserving of the support it needs in achieving its ends (G 4:430). Similarly, the imperfect duty to promote the happiness of others (example 4) can be understood as grounded in the requirement to recognize other rational beings as one's equals and so to treat their rational nature as deserving of assistance by promoting some of their permissible ends in addition to one's own (G 4:430). Both imperfect duties derive from the fact that given the kind of limited, dependent rational beings we are, our rational nature cannot flourish without efforts to support the natural abilities on which its efficacy depends, and to assist in the promotion of one another's ends.

FH does a nice job of making clear that not all acts of a given type (e.g., drinking alcohol) will automatically be wrong if one maxim of that act type is. What matters morally is whether the maxim of the action is one that shows proper respect for rational nature. The notion that morality has essentially to do with respect for persons and their capacity to make choices for themselves is one of the most influential and compelling ideas in Kant's ethics.

Of course, however, there are questions about FH. Most obviously, it is far from clear what respect for every given rational being demands of us in every situation. Kant recognizes this, and in his *Metaphysics of Morals* "Doctrine of Virtue" includes many "casuistical questions," which help readers gain practice in thinking about what respect for their own or others' rational nature demands. This indeterminacy may not be a flaw in Kant's theory, but simply a fact about morality: it may be difficult to figure out exactly what proper respect amounts to in certain cases, even if one is sure that proper respect is morally required. There are also questions about what it means (both literally and practically) for Kant to say that rational nature has "absolute worth" or "dignity." This claim is usually taken to imply that one cannot equate the value of a rational being with the value of anything else, or count five rational beings as together more valuable than four rational beings. But then how do we reconcile these ideas with common practices such as making tradeoffs between the efficiency of certain speed limits relative to the number of lives lost, which seems to involve both counting the loss of more human lives as worse than the loss of fewer, and considering the protection of human life something that can be weighed against convenience? Is the preceding way of thinking about the value of human life in conflict with FH, and so wrong? Are these ways of thinking, despite initial appearances, compatible with recognizing the dignity of rational nature? Or do these ways of thinking somehow suggest a failure inherent in FH?

Kant sets forth two more versions of the categorical imperative. The formula of autonomy (FA), which Kant says follows from FUL/N and FH (G 4:431), presents "the idea of the will of every rational being as a will giving universal law" and commands us "so to act that the will could at the same time regard itself as giving through its maxims universal laws" (G 4:434). The formula of the kingdom of ends (FKE), which Kant says follows from FA, presents the idea of a "systematic union of different rational beings through common laws," with "all ends combined in a systematic whole (including both rational beings as ends in themselves, and also the special ends which each may propose to himself)" (G 4:433), and commands us to "act according to the maxims of a member of a merely possible kingdom of ends legislating in it universally" (G 4:439).

FA is similar to FUL/N in its explicit reference to universal laws. But FA goes beyond FUL/N in saying that the universal laws to which the will conforms must be self-legislated. It takes from FH the recognition of the value of rational nature, which rationally commands respect. But FA calls attention to an aspect of rational nature not highlighted by FH, autonomy. Kant defines "autonomy of the will" as "that property of it by which it is a law unto itself (independent of any property of the objects of volition)" (G 4:440). As we will see more clearly in Section 3, Kant takes autonomy to involve not only the will's giving itself a law, but also its being able to motivate itself out of an interest in that law for its own sake. A heteronomous will would be ruled by something outside it, independent of its own rational standards, such as self-love or fear of God. Such a will could be motivated to obey moral principles only by appeal to interests in contingently good ends, such as the desire for physical pleasure or a successful career. So heteronomous legislation can yield only hypothetical imperatives, not categorical ones. Kant describes all moral theories except for his own as failing to explain the categorical nature of moral obligation—and to locate the supreme principle of morality—precisely because they failed to see morality as autonomously legislated (G 4:441, 444).

Kant often describes rational agents as autonomous, meaning that they have the capacity for self-legislation, that they are subject to self-legislated moral demands. Kant also sees the CI as demanding that agents act autonomously, obeying our self-given moral requirements. One must be autonomous in the first sense to be subject to the demand to realize autonomy in the second sense.[1]

While FA offers agents an image of themselves as legislators of moral laws, FKE offers agents an image of themselves as members of a community of co-legislators of these laws. FKE presents agents with an abstract ideal of a community of rational beings regarded as ends in themselves, harmonizing their pursuits of their ends with respect for their own and one another's dignity, and with others' pursuits of their own ends. FKE requires agents to think of maxims not in isolation from one another, but as part of a system.[2] FKE seems to prefigure both images Kant uses in his political writings about the coordination of the pursuit of chosen ends in harmony with everyone's external freedom within a state (**MM 6:230-31**), and those he uses in his religious writing about how members of ethical communities can aide one another in their pursuits of happiness and (less directly) virtue (Rel 6:93-100).

Given the obvious differences in the formulations of the CI, it is natural to ask what relations are supposed to hold among them.

---

1 See Appendix I for Sidgwick's criticism that Kant improperly moves between these two notions of freedom (or autonomy).
2 For a discussion of FKE, see Chapter 3 of Thomas E. Hill Jr., *Dignity and Practical Reason* (Ithaca, NY: Cornell UP, 1992).

Kant says "the three modes of presenting the principle of morality that have been adduced are at bottom only so many formulae of the very same law, and each unites itself in the other two. There is, however, a difference among them, but it is subjectively rather than objectively practical, intended, namely, to bring an idea of reason nearer to intuition (by means of a certain analogy) and thereby nearer to feeling" (G 4:436). He then describes FUL/N as one formulation, which expresses the form of universalizability morality requires a maxim to have; FH as a second, conveying that each maxim must, to be moral, treat rational nature as an end in itself; and (apparently, though this is open to dispute) FA/FKE as a third, which conveys that "all maxims ought, by their own legislation, to harmonize with a possible kingdom of ends as with a kingdom of nature" (G 4:436). Commentators have found this passage less than conclusive, however. They have continued to wonder precisely what the relation among the formulations is supposed to be,[1] and even questioned whether it makes sense to think of there being only three main formulations of the CI (rather than four).[2] There are also questions about which formulation Kant refers to at particular times: some passages seem ambiguous between FUL/N and FA (e.g., importantly, at G 4:436-37).[3] I will say a few words here about three ways of understanding the relation among the formulations.

One approach to the relation among the formulations of the CI has been to see each (main) formulation as self-sufficient, containing the full CI, expressed in a particular way. On this view, the different formulations are all equal and have the same (objective) content, but are subjectively more useful in some ways than others, revealing different aspects of the CI with more clarity in some formulations. This first approach gains support from Kant's apparent (though perhaps misunderstood) use of FUL/N and FH to explain the moral standing of certain maxims of actions and ends (G 4:421-23, 429-30), as well as from Kant's most explicit claim (G 4:436, quoted above) about the relations among the

---

1 For a discussion of ways to understand the relations among the formulae, see Chapter 7 of Onora O'Neill, *Constructions of Reason* (Cambridge: Cambridge UP, 1989).

2 Paul Guyer argues that Kant sets out four distinct formulations, all of which are necessary for showing how the CI is possible. See "The Possibility of the Categorical Imperative," *Kant on Freedom, Law, and Happiness* (Cambridge: Cambridge UP, 2000).

3 See chapter 5 of Allen W. Wood, *Kant's Ethical Thought*, especially 182-90.

formulations. A problem with this account is that it does not seem to do justice to the progressive nature of Kant's argument, and to the fact that FUL/N seems a thinner and more provisional expression of the CI than FA/FKE. Moreover, some commentators and translators would say a better translation of the above passage would read not "*each* unites in itself the other two" but "*one* unites in itself the other two" (my emphasis).[1] Yet without having a view of the philosophy, the matter of how best to translate the passage is not clear; so translation cannot settle the question.

A second approach says they are all the same law in that *together* all of them express the CI; each articulates a part of it, but none alone captures the whole. This approach fits with only part of Kant's explicit statement about the relation among the formulations, that is, with the suggestion that they have different subjective employments. Yet it fits well with the way Kant seems to draw the formulations together after that (at G 4:437-39), combining them in ways that suggest each alone expresses only part of the CI, and that a full understanding of the CI requires all of them.

A third approach sees the formulations as progressive, with FUL/N telling us something about the CI (the form it requires maxims to have), FH telling us something more (about the required end), and FA/FKE, telling us everything. On this view, FA/FKE is complete, containing FUL/N and FH within it.[2] This last approach gains plausibility from Kant's progressive style of argument in Section 2; from his description of FA/FKE as conveying a "complete determination" of all maxims in terms of form, matter, and systematic totality; from considering the ascending sophistication and inclusiveness of the formulations themselves; and from Kant's focus on autonomy as "the supreme principle of morality" in Section 2. This approach is compatible with finding FUL/N and FH useful in certain capacities, though not the fullest articulations of the CI. Though this last interpretation has much to be said for it, support for it is not conclusive. Readers are encouraged to evaluate these, and consider other possible relations, themselves. They are also cautioned to keep the issue in perspective: the latter parts of Section 2, in which Kant recombines various parts of the formulations in different ways, emphasize that for Kant universalizability, rational nature as an

---

1 See Wood's translation of the *Groundwork*, 54.
2 See, for example, chapter 5 of Wood, *Kant's Ethical Thought*, and chapter 7 of O'Neill, *Constructions of Reason*.

end in itself, self-legislation, and systematic harmony are necessary elements of the full articulation of what the CI requires of our maxims; how many ways one chooses to articulate these requirements seems far less crucial than the requirements themselves.

By the end of Section 2, Kant takes himself to have investigated the supreme moral principle, showing that, for beings like us, it is a categorical imperative, and setting forth various versions of this CI. But he does not think he has established this principle as binding on us: this is the task for Section 3.

Section 3

In Section 3, Kant seeks to establish the supreme moral principle by showing that the CI is valid for rational agents—that it is rationally binding on us, and that we are capable of obeying it for its own sake (i.e., that we can act from duty). In other words, Section 3 must show us that morality is not "a phantom of the brain," as it would be if there were no categorically binding, supreme moral principle in which more particular moral judgments and choices might be grounded (G 4:445).

Kant's main argument can be seen as having three parts: an argument to show that the moral law is the law of the free will; an argument to show that rational beings must regard themselves as free; and the conclusion, that rational beings must regard themselves as subject to the moral law.[1]

Kant argues for the first premise in the first three paragraphs of Section 3. First, he explains his *negative* conception of freedom as a will's ability to bring about effects in the world without itself being determined by "foreign causes" (impulses, feelings, or anything else external to reason). He then argues that any negatively free will must also be free in the *positive* sense, i.e., autonomous. According to Kant, the will is a kind of rational causality, capable of producing changes in the world. We cannot think of a will as lawless, because the very concept of cause implies a law-governed relation between cause and effect. A will that is negatively free cannot be heteronomous, e.g., having as its law "the law of nature," for then its causality would be determined by alien causes—either directly by immediately determining the will to action, or indirectly by determining the will to ends—precisely what

---

1   See Korsgaard, "Morality as Freedom" and "Creating the Kingdom of Ends" in *Creating the Kingdom of Ends*.

negative freedom precludes. Thus, a will free in the negative sense must also be free in the positive sense, capable of determining itself through reason alone, and hence autonomous. We already know from Section 2 that the law the autonomous will gives itself is the moral law. So the law of the free will is the moral law.

Kant gives his initial argument for the second premise, that we must regard ourselves as free, and therefore as subject to the moral law, in the fourth paragraph. There he claims that all rational beings invariably and unavoidably act "under the idea of freedom" and thus "from a practical point of view [are] really free" (G 4:448). Whenever we decide what to do, even about the most trivial matter, we implicitly take ourselves to be free causes, determining our own wills, aiming to make certain things happen in the world. The assumption of freedom is implicit in the deliberation and choice of every rational being. We are committed to this "practical" standpoint simply by our status as rational beings. This does not mean we cannot also think of ourselves as causally determined. Kant holds that from the "theoretical" standpoint of science and observation, we can explain human action as determined by such things as psychological, physical, and social factors. What he insists upon, however, and what is crucial for this argument, is that this theoretical standpoint neither removes the need for the practical standpoint, nor refutes the presupposition of freedom inherent in that standpoint. Kant describes us as part of the "sensible world" insofar as we think of ourselves as empirically knowable, understandable in terms of determinism according to natural laws, and as part of the "intelligible world" insofar as we think of ourselves as rational and free, not comprehensible in empirical and deterministic terms (G 4:447, 451).[1]

Thus, Kant can conclude that, since we inevitably ascribe freedom to ourselves, and since the moral law is the law of the free will, we must take ourselves to be bound by the moral law.

Two related aspects of this argument that have engaged commentators are our interest in the moral law, and the alleged circle in Kant's explanation of that interest. Part of the question of whether the moral law obligates us has to do with whether and how we can

---

1 Kant's distinction between the practical and theoretical standpoints (or the intelligible world and the world of sense) is one of the most controversial and provocative aspects of his philosophy. Henry E. Allison discusses it in relation to Kant's ethics throughout *Kant's Theory of Freedom* (Cambridge: Cambridge UP, 1990).

"take an interest in it," i.e., be motivated to obey it for its own sake. We are motivated to follow hypothetical imperatives because of our inclination-based desires for the ends that ground them; what motivates us to follow the CI, which so often demands the frustration of our inclination-based pursuits (G 4:417, 419-20, 449)? Kant's answer is that we take an interest in the moral law because our standing as autonomous, rational beings, by virtue of which the moral law is valid for us, makes us "feel our worth" as beings with dignity (G 4:449, 454). It is in so far as we regard ourselves as able to act on self-given principles of reason that we regard ourselves as ends in themselves; and it is this very freedom which makes us subject to the law. So our interest in our own autonomy and dignity explains our interest in the law (G 4:450, CprR 5:72-81).

But Kant worries that his reasoning is circular: we appeal to our freedom to explain our interest in self-legislation and our obligation to the moral law; yet this freedom simply *is* moral self-legislation, interest in and obligation to which we are trying to explain (G 4:450). Kant escapes the circle by saying that our freedom (or our membership in the "intelligible world") can be seen not only in reason's practical exercise but also in its *theoretical* employment. In reasons's capacity to produce "ideas" (such as God or the soul), the objects of which do not correspond to any possible object of sensible experience, we find a capacity we cannot conceive as operating through natural necessity, as part of the "sensible world." Since we can recognize reason's freedom in its theoretical employment without presupposing the moral law, we have a non-circular way to argue for our freedom, and to argue from this freedom to the validity of the moral law for us (G 4:450-53).

There is disagreement about how best to describe Kant's strategy for breaking the circle, as well as how successful the strategy is.[1] Kant's *Critique of Practical Reason* argues in the opposite direction from Section 3 of the *Groundwork*. In the second *Critique*, Kant begins with the assumption that morality binds us, and argues that we become aware of our freedom through that obligation. In the second *Critique*, Kant seems to see no need to appeal to the freedom of reason in its theoretical employment.[2] Some

---

1   See chapter 12 of Allison, *Kant's Theory of Freedom*, and "On the Presumed Gap in the Derivation of the Categorical Imperative" in *Idealism and Freedom* (Cambridge: Cambridge UP, 1996); also see chapter 3 of O'Neill, *Constructions of Reason*.

2   See Lewis White Beck, *A Commentary on Kant's Critique of Practical Reason* (Chicago: U of Chicago P, 1960).

have taken Kant's strategy in the second *Critique* as an indication that Kant himself saw his *Groundwork* argument as a failure. This is an important issue, for Kant's "establishment" of the supreme moral principle is complete only if this synthetic argument, connecting rational nature with the self-legislated moral law via freedom and the intelligible world, succeeds—be it in *Groundwork* Section 3, or elsewhere.

Kant's Ethics Beyond the *Groundwork*

There is much more to Kant's ethics than the *Groundwork*. Some important parts of this "much more" are contained in the appended excerpts from Kant's other works. I will conclude this introduction by pointing the reader toward a few ideas that help give a more complete picture of Kant's ethics.

First, *Kant's normative ethics is a system of duties,* which provides fairly concrete, substantive guidance about the purposes one should strive for and the kinds of maxims one may and may not act on. The *Metaphysics of Morals* contains both a "Doctrine of Right," comprising the foundational principles for duties of justice and explicating our "innate right to freedom," and a "Doctrine of Virtue," containing a taxonomy of duties of virtue, which can be only self-legislated and self-compelled. The universal principle of "right" (or justice) is, "Any action is *right* if it can coexist with everyone's freedom of action in accordance with a universal law, or if on its maxims the freedom of choice of each can coexist with everyone's freedom in accordance with a universal law" (**MM 6:230**).[1] The supreme principle of the doctrine of virtue is, "Act in accordance with a maxim of *ends* that it can be a universal law for everyone to have." Kant goes on, "In accordance with this principle a human being is an end for himself as well as for others, and it is not enough that he is not authorized to use either himself or others merely as a means (since he could then still be indifferent to them); it is in itself his duty to make the human being as such his end" (**MM 6:395**). Indeed, in nearly all of his explanations of particular duties of virtue, the requirement to make the human being one's end is at the forefront.

Kant provides a fairly straightforward, easy-to-learn collection

---

1   On the relation between this principle and the CI, see Guyer, "Kant's Deductions of the Principles of Right" in *Kant's Metaphysics of Morals: Interpretive Essays*, ed. Mark Timmons (New York: Oxford UP, 2002).

of duties of virtue in the "Doctrine of Virtue."[1] We have duties to ourselves that demand we use our physical selves only in keeping with its reason-supporting role (perfect duties to oneself as an animal and moral being), prohibiting suicide and self-mutilation, sexual self-degradation, gluttony, and drunkenness; duties that demand not undermining or insulting our rational nature through maxims of lying, avarice, or servility (perfect duties to oneself as a moral being only); duties that require us to strive to develop our natural talents in ways that fit our interests and abilities, as well as to strive for virtue and full completion of all our duties (both of which follow from the obligatory end of our own perfection). We have duties to others to refrain from arrogance, defamation, and ridicule (duties of respect); duties to show others beneficence, gratitude, and sympathy (duties of love, which follow from the obligatory end of the happiness of others); and duties to refrain from malice, envy, and ingratitude (vices contrary to duties of love). Kant explicates all these duties as following from the requirement to respect rational beings, together with facts about human nature.

With a rough sense of what her duties are, and what makes these various types of maxims vicious or virtuous, an agent can go through many day to day decisions knowing what sorts of behavior to avoid or cultivate. When in doubt about whether an act is right or wrong, she need not use an abstract, all-purpose decision procedure, such as FUL/N is taken by some commentators to be. She will often be able to ask much more specific questions about her maxims in reference to particular duties of virtue—e.g., "is my manner servile in this letter to my former professor, or simply appreciative and polite?" In other words, through its system of duties, Kant's normative ethics provides a context for confronting substantive moral questions that is far more concrete than anything one could infer from the *Groundwork*.[2]

---

1 See Appendix E, **MM 6:391-94, 418-20, 422-24, 443, 448-50, 457.**
2 Appendix E does not contain many of Kant's most detailed expositions of particular duties of virtue, but provides his explanations of different kinds of duties included in his taxonomy, in addition to Kant's explanations of virtue, obligatory ends, and a number of more general aspects of his normative ethics. The most exhaustive exploration of Kant's *Metaphysics of Morals*, and Kant's arguments for the duties contained therein, is Mary J. Gregor, *Laws of Freedom: A Study of Kant's Method of Applying the Categorical Imperative in the* Metaphysik der Sitten (Oxford: Basil Blackwell, 1963).

Second, *respect for rational nature and the value of autonomy are central not only in the Groundwork but throughout Kant's ethics.* It is already clear in the *Groundwork* that the autonomy of rational beings is the central, fundamental value in Kant's ethical theory. This theme is developed throughout his other ethical writings, as well as writings in related areas. All our moral duties are autonomously legislated. Duties of virtue are duties that can be compelled only by the agent herself. They aim (to varying degrees) to maintain and promote the agent's inner freedom. And Kant grounds them all in the requirement to respect one's own or others' rational nature—rational nature of which the defining property is the capacity for self-legislation (autonomy). More dramatically, Kant describes autonomy as our "higher vocation" (CprR 5:87) and "proper self" (G 4:461) and claims that the intelligible world it makes us part of gives us an identity and importance far beyond what we could ever have as mere animals (CprR 5:162). Similarly, in Kant's writings on aesthetics and nature, Kant says that in the face of the most terrible, awesome, "sublime" objects—such as volcanoes, tsunami, and glaciers—we simultaneously feel vulnerable as animals and powerful as rational beings: despite the threat nature poses to us as animals, "we regard nature's might as yet not having such dominance over us as persons, that we should have to bow if our highest principles were at stake and we had to choose between upholding or abandoning them" (CJ 5:262). Our wills are immune to nature's forces. In writing about rearing and educating children, Kant presents autonomy, not obedience, as the ultimate aim. One should steer the child to appreciate the dignity of herself and other rational beings and the authority of morality, and recognize that she herself is a legislator of moral law (E 9:83-121). Finally, Kant's social and political philosophy is also fundamentally informed by the value of rational nature and autonomy. In "An Answer to the Question: 'What is Enlightenment?',"[1] Kant urges adults to think for themselves, and argues that for social progress to take place, people must have the freedom to share their thoughts publicly. Progress demands not (heteronomously) automatically deferring to external authorities; it demands questioning the status quo, sharing one's doubts and concerns about the government and other institutions (though not in ways that violate obligations one has in particular private capacities, e.g., through offices one

---

1 Included in its entirety in Appendix A. Also see Kant's "Supreme Principle of Right" (MM 6:230-31), Appendix E.

holds). Thus, Kant's views on the importance of civil freedoms reflects the value he attributes to the autonomy of rational agents.

Third, *Kant has a rich conception of virtue, combining the realization of autonomy through self-mastery with the maintenance and development of many of one's natural inclinations and feelings.* Kant describes virtue as a human being's commitment and "strength of will" to do the right thing out of respect for the moral law, even in the face of inclinations and impulses tempting her to do otherwise (**MM 6:394**). Thus, for Kant, virtue centrally involves self-constraint of a distinctly moral kind. After reading the *Groundwork* discussion of the good will and moral worth, few people are surprised that Kant associates control over one's· emotions and inclinations, "self-mastery," with virtue (MM 6:407-409). What surprises many readers is that Kant's conception of the virtuous person is of someone who protects and cultivates many of these feelings and inclinations. To be sure, some feelings and impulses may be best ignored or squelched, and the virtuous agent stands ready and able to do so. But on the whole, Kant sees our animal nature as providing us with feelings and impulses that can, when handled properly, assist us in our fulfillment of our duties. Sympathy, for example, is a feeling that Kant thinks we have a duty to cultivate due to its usefulness in making us sensitive and responsive to the needs of others (**MM 6:457**). Indeed, because Kant so values feelings such as love and sympathy for their moral usefulness, and because he thinks we feel these emotions for nonrational as well as for rational beings, Kant argues that we have duties to be kind and not cruel to nonhuman animals; for cruelty to them tends to erode the tender feelings so helpful in our duties to other people, and kindness to foster those feelings (**MM 6:443**). Love and sympathy cannot themselves ground duties, or take the place of respect for the law as the fundamental moral motive. But they can make us more effective and eager to do what duty demands, and we should encourage them in that capacity. And contrary to the picture Kant paints of the misanthropist helping others out of duty while lacking in feelings of love, Kant portrays his virtuous agent as someone who gets pleasure out of helping others—not only because there is a moral satisfaction in doing the right thing because it is right, but because he naturally comes to care about and rejoice in the happiness of those he helps, because he has fostered these feelings of love and sympathy in himself.[1]

---

1   On Kant's theory of virtue, see Lara Denis, "Kant's Concept of Virtue" in *The Cambridge Companion to Kant* (second edition) ed. Paul Guyer (Cambridge: Cambridge UP, forthcoming).

Fourth, *Kant's ethics includes a conception of "the highest good,"* *which in turn provides an argument for the rationality of religious belief.* One thing one would not expect from Kant's ethics from reading only the *Groundwork* is that it includes the notion of an ultimate end, beyond a good will, virtue, or autonomy, that we are to see our lives as striving toward. This ultimate end is the highest good: the complete object of pure practical reason, the systematic unity of all ends that reason takes to be good as ends. For Kant, the highest good is composed of virtue, which is unconditionally good, and happiness (the satisfaction of one's wants, wishes, and needs), which is conditionally good—i.e., good when enjoyed in morally permissible ways by virtuous agents (**CprR 5:110-11**). Kant uses this notion of the highest good to argue for the rationality of belief in God. He argues that because reason forms this idea of an ultimate end for our moral efforts, we must find a way to see such an end as capable of realization; otherwise, morality would seem to point us toward a fraudulent end, and thus strike us as itself fraudulent; but we cannot see how human agency alone could bring about the highest good; only by postulating the existence of God can we believe in the possibility of the highest good's realization; because no argument can show that God does not exist, we are entitled to believe in God's existence on practical grounds (**CprR 5:120-26**). This argument is interesting not merely because it allows only *belief* in God, not claiming to *know* that God exists (which would require a theoretical cognition which Kant argues we cannot have) (CprR 5:134-41; CpuR A631-42/B659-670, A826-30/B854-58), but also because it makes religious belief depend on morality, rather than morality depend on religion (Rel 6:5-6).

Fifth, *Kant's normative ethics draws on ideas about human nature,* *including the importance of community to human beings.* If we are to know what our duties are as human moral agents, we must apply the categorical imperative to us. This requires figuring out what it takes to respect rational nature in human beings. That in turn requires understanding our various natural predispositions, needs, capacities, and vulnerabilities—right down to biological and psychological facts about us. It is important to know that, for example, we can be physically harmed in ways that impair our efficacy as agents, that our natural talents do not develop without active cultivation, and that many things crucial to the satisfaction of our natural needs cannot be achieved without aid from others. And if we want to have a rough list of duties, we need to know what sorts of things human beings commonly want to do and why. For example, we tend to like sex, food, and drink so much that we can easily find ourselves indulging in those pleasures for enjoyment, without regard to what self-respect requires. So though Kant does not think empirical research can lead us to the supreme moral principle, he thinks empirical information is indispensable for figuring out what this principle actually demands of us in our treatment of ourselves and one another.

Moreover, if we want to know what it is to be a morally good human being, we need to know not only what our duties are, but what form autonomy's full realization takes in humans. Indeed, Kant thinks his notion of the *radical evil* in human nature is crucial for understanding why we find morality such a struggle, and so why virtue requires such self-mastery. Kant's view is that human beings find it hard to do the right thing not simply because we have needs and inclinations, but also because we have made our fundamental maxim a less than complete observance of the moral law: the human being "is conscious of the moral law and yet has incorporated into his maxim the (occasional) deviation from it" (**Rel 6:32**). Kant does not attempt to explain why we have done this; indeed, he does not think an explanation is possible (Rel 6:43). But he does think this notion of the radical evil in human nature is helpful for understanding the nature of virtue for human beings—all our day to day struggles to do the right thing can be seen as manifestations or consequences of this radical evil.

Finally, much of what Kant thinks we need to understand about ourselves and our moral predicament has to do with our social nature. Community is important in Kant's thinking not just because we have to find a way to pursue our ends without impinging on others. Kant sees our social drives as playing crucial roles in shaping our desires and our conceptions of happiness. Indeed, Kant remarks that we judge ourselves happy in relation to others; it is a comparative judgment (Rel 6:27). Many of our duties of respect and vices contrary to duties of love obviously consist in requirements to thwart some of the darker tendencies of our nature to feel good about ourselves by, for example, putting others down, lording power over them, or mocking them, or our jealous desire not to acknowledge our gratitude for others. When Kant insists that we must form ethical communities in order to help one another in our moral progress, much of the reason for this is our propensity to drag one another down into vice if we do not make a concerted effort to work toward the contrary (Rel

6:93-98). The struggle against evil requires us to work together, because we invariably tempt others to evil if we aren't so united against it. We are drawn to other human beings for love, but also for much darker reasons. Kant takes our "unsocial sociability" to play a deep and far-reaching role in creating the context for the moral life of human beings. Thus, though the focus in the *Groundwork* is "pure" moral philosophy, Kant's full moral theory involves much empirical speculation. Indeed, Kant's philosophy of history cites unsocial sociability and the competition it inspires as powerful engines of progress.[1]

While this sort of empirical theorizing is necessary for a full Kantian moral theory, and while some of what Kant says is insightful and provocative, one can deny many of Kant's specific claims about human nature, or about the nature of a particular sex or nation, and still have a genuinely Kantian moral theory. But alas, further development of Kant's normative ethics is beyond the scope of this introduction.

---

1 Wood discusses Kant's theories of human nature (and to a lesser degree, history) in chapters 6-8 of *Kant's Ethical Thought*. For a study of the relation between Kant's ethics and his philosophies of religion, education, history, art, and human nature, see Robert Louden, *Kant's Impure Ethics: From Rational Beings to Human Beings* (New York: Oxford UP, 2000).

Immanuel Kant: A Brief Chronology

1724	Immanuel Kant is born in Königsberg, Prussia (now Kaliningrad, Russia), to Anna Regina Kant (1697-1737) and Johann Georg Kant (1682-1746).
1732	Kant enters the *Collegium Fridericianum*.
1740	Kant matriculates at the University of Königsberg. Frederick William I dies. Frederick II (the Great) becomes king of Prussia.
1748-54	Kant works as a private tutor.
1749	*Thoughts on the True Estimation of the Living Forces* (Kant's first book).
1755	Kant begins lecturing at the University of Königsberg.
1762-64	Kant teaches Johann Gottfried Herder.
1763	*The Only Possible Argument in Support of a Demonstration of the Existence of God.*
1764	*Observations on the Feeling of the Beautiful and Sublime. Inquiry Concerning the Distinctness of the Principles of Natural Theology and Morality* (prize essay for the Berlin Academy).
1766	*Dreams of a Spirit-seer.* Kant begins corresponding with Moses Mendelssohn.
1770	Kant is appointed Professor in Logic and Metaphysics at the University of Königsberg. "On the Form and Principles of the Sensible and Intelligible World" (inaugural dissertation).
1781	*Critique of Pure Reason* (first edition).
1783	*Prolegomena to Any Future Metaphysics.*
1784	"Idea for a Universal History of Mankind." "An Answer to the Question, 'What is Enlightenment?'"
1785	*Groundwork for the Metaphysics of Morals.* "On the Wrongful Publication of Books." "On the Definition of the Concept of a Human Race."
1786	*Metaphysical Foundations of Natural Science.* "Conjectural Beginning of the Human Race." "What is Orientation in Thinking?" Kant becomes an external member of the Berlin Academy of the Sciences.

	Frederick the Great dies.

Frederick the Great dies.
Frederick William II becomes king of Prussia.
1787   *Critique of Pure Reason* (second edition).
1788   *Critique of Practical Reason.*
"On the Use of Teleological Principles in Philosophy."
The king issues two edicts on religion.
1789   The French Revolution begins.
1790   *Critique of the Power of Judgment.*
1791   "On the Failure of All Philosophical Attempts at Theodicy."
1793   "Concerning Radical Evil."
Religion within the Limits of Reason Alone (first edition).
"On the Common Saying, 'This May Be True in Theory, but It Does Not Apply in Practice.'"
The king issues a stricter edict on religion.
1794   *Religion within the Limits of Reason Alone* (second edition).
"Something on the Influence of the Moon on the Climate."
"The End of All Things."
Kant becomes a member of the Petersburg Academy.
Kant is censored by the king.
1795   *Toward Perpetual Peace* (first edition).
Kant corresponds with Friedrich von Schiller.
1796   *Toward Perpetual Peace* (second edition).
Kant gives his final lecture.
1797   *Metaphysical Principles of the Doctrine of Right.*
Metaphysical Principles of the Doctrine of Virtue.
"On a Presumed Right to Lie from Philanthropic Motives."
Frederick William II dies.
Frederick William III becomes king of Prussia.
1798   *The Conflict of the Faculties.*
Anthropology from a Pragmatic Point of View.
"On Turning Out Books."
1800   *Logic* (edited by Gottlob Benjamin Jäsche).
1802   *Physical Geography* (edited by Friedrich Theodor Rink).
1803   *On Education* (edited by Rink).
1804   Kant dies.

A Note on the Text

This translation of Kant's *Groundwork for the Metaphysics of Morals* primarily represents the work of Thomas K. Abbott. Abbott's *A Critique of Practical Reason and Other Works on the Theory of Ethics*, first published in 1873 by Longman's, Green, and Company, includes Kant's *Gundlegung zur Metaphysik der Sitten*, which Abbott translated as *Fundamental principles of the metaphysic of morals*.

I have made many, mostly minor, alterations to Abbott's venerable translation. I have updated spelling, eliminated some anachronistic turns of phrase, and made some changes in word choice to reflect current preferences among Kant scholars. A noteworthy example of the last sort of change is my translating *"Triebfeder"* as "incentive," though Abbott usually translates it as "spring" (or "spring of action"). The more literal "spring" (as in the mainspring of a watch, clock, or other mechanism), has the virtue of clearly conveying that a *Triebfeder* is something *within* an agent that moves her to act or causes her to desire something, not a feature of an object that arouses in her a desire for that object (such as the "financial incentives" advertised by car dealers). Nevertheless, its consistency with the appended texts, as well as with most current translations of and secondary literature on Kant's ethics, made "incentive" preferable for this edition. Although I have made some additional semantic changes simply to suit my ear—and so perhaps also the ears of contemporary readers—I have altered the syntax only in the rare cases in which doing so seemed necessary for facilitating readers' comprehension.

I have retained some but not all of Abbott's explanatory notes and have added some notes of my own. The choice about which notes to add and eliminate has been driven by the aim of this Broadview edition of the *Groundwork*: to provide a useful introduction to Kant's ethics generally, and to the *Groundwork* in particular. Several of my notes point the reader to relevant appendices later in the book. The reader should have no trouble distinguishing among Kant's, Abbott's, and my notes. Kant's notes are followed by his initials in square brackets, "[I.K.]"; Abbott's notes are themselves in square brackets; and my own are unmarked. In the appendices, my own notes remain unmarked, and both Kant's and translators' notes are indicated by their initials in square brackets.

There is one further remark I should make about my revisions, concerning marginal page numbers. Abbott's translation is based on the 1838 Rosenkranz and Schubert edition of Kant's *Grundlegung*. Rather than insert those page numbers in the margins, however, I have provided the page numbers to the Prussian Academy edition of Kant's works. I have done this because it is the Prussian Academy edition that is referred to almost universally in contemporary Kant scholarship. Thus, students will be able to read articles and books on Kant and trace the page citations from those works to this translation of the *Groundwork*. Moreover, I have included the Prussian Academy page numbers for the appended selections from Kant's works, including those in which the translator used a different edition of Kant's works in German. Note that Prussian Academy pagination includes volume and page number (e.g., 4:450 for volume 4, page 450); I have included the volume number only at the beginning of each selection.

GROUNDWORK
FOR THE METAPHYSICS OF
MORALS

Preface [4:387]

Ancient Greek philosophy was divided into three sciences: **physics, ethics,** and **logic**. This division is perfectly suitable to the nature of the thing; and the only improvement that can be made in it is to add the principle on which it is based, so that we may both satisfy ourselves of its completeness, and also be able to determine correctly the necessary subdivisions.

All rational cognition is either *material* or *formal*: the former considers some object, the latter is concerned only with the form of the understanding and of reason itself, and with the universal laws of thought in general without distinction of its objects. Formal philosophy is called logic.[1] Material philosophy, however, which has to do with determinate objects and the laws to which they are subject, is again twofold; for these laws are either laws of **nature** or of **freedom**. The science of the former is **physics**, that of the latter, **ethics**; they are also called natural philosophy and moral philosophy respectively.

Logic cannot have any empirical part—that is, a part in which the universal and necessary laws of thought should rest on grounds taken from experience; otherwise, it would not be logic, that is, a canon for the understanding or the reason, valid for all thought, and capable of demonstration. Natural and moral philosophy, by contrast, can each have their empirical part, since the former has to determine the laws of nature as an object of experience, the latter the laws of the human will, so far as it is affected by nature; the former, however, being laws according to which [388] everything does happen, the latter, laws according to which everything ought to happen. Ethics, however, must also consider the conditions under which what ought to happen frequently does not.

We may call all philosophy *empirical*, so far as it is based on grounds of experience; on the other hand, that which delivers its doctrines from *a priori*[2] principles alone we may call *pure* philosophy. When the latter is merely formal, it is *logic*; if it is restricted to definite objects of the understanding, it is *metaphysics*.

In this way there arises the idea of a twofold metaphysics, a

---

1 See Kant, *Logic* (1800), edited by Jäsche.
2 *A priori* principles are inherent in and revealed through the exercise of reason. They are independent of any particular experience or observation.

GROUNDWORK FOR THE METAPHYSICS OF MORALS 49

metaphysics of nature[1] and a *metaphysics of morals.*[2] Physics will thus have an empirical and also a rational part. It is the same with ethics; but here the empirical part might have the special name of *practical anthropology*,[3] the name *morality* being appropriated to the rational part.

All trades, arts, and handiworks have gained by division of labor, namely, when instead of one man doing everything, each confines himself to a certain kind of work distinct from others in the treatment it requires, so as to be able to perform it with greater facility and in the greatest perfection. Where the different kinds of work are not so distinguished and divided, where everyone is a jack-of-all-trades, there manufacturers remain still in the greatest barbarism. It might deserve to be considered whether pure philosophy in all its parts does not require a person specially devoted to it, and whether it would not be better for the whole business of science if those who, to please the tastes of the public, are wont to blend the rational and empirical elements together, mixed in all sorts of proportions unknown to themselves, and who call themselves independent thinkers, giving the name of hair-splitters to those who apply themselves to the rational part only—if these, I say, were warned not to carry on two employments together which differ widely in the treatment they demand, for each of which perhaps a special talent is required, and the combination of which in one person only produces bunglers. But I only ask here whether the nature of science does not require that we should always carefully separate the empirical from the rational part, and prefix to physics proper (empirical physics) a metaphysics of nature, and to practical anthropology, a metaphysics of morals, which must be carefully cleared of everything empirical so that we may know how much can be accomplished by pure reason in both cases, and from what sources it draws this its *a priori* teaching, and that whether the latter inquiry is conducted by all moralists (whose name is legion), or only by some who feel a calling to it.

As my concern here is with moral philosophy, I limit the question suggested to this: whether it is not of the utmost necessity to construct a pure moral philosophy, perfectly cleared of everything

[389]

---

1 See Kant, *Metaphysical Foundations of Natural Science* (1786).
2 See Kant, *Metaphysics of Morals* (containing the "Doctrine of Right" and the "Doctrine of Virtue") (1797). See Appendix E for excerpts.
3 Kant, *Anthropology from a Pragmatic Point of View* (1798).

which is only empirical and which belongs to anthropology? For that such a philosophy must be possible is evident from the common idea of duty and of the moral laws. Everyone must admit that if a law is to have moral force, that is, to be the basis of an obligation, it must carry with it absolute necessity; that, for example, the precept, "You ought not to lie," is not valid for human beings alone, as if other rational beings had no need to observe it; and so with all the other moral laws properly so called; that therefore, the basis of obligation must not be sought in the nature of the human being, or in the circumstances in the world in which he is placed, but *a priori* simply in the concepts of pure reason; and although any other precept which is founded on principles of mere experience may be in certain respects universal, yet in as far as it rests even in the least degree on an empirical basis, perhaps only as to a motive, such a precept, while it may be a practical rule, can never be called a moral law.

Thus not only are moral laws with their principles essentially distinguished from every other kind of practical cognition in which there is anything empirical, but all moral philosophy rests wholly on its pure part. When applied to human beings, it does not borrow the least thing from acquaintance with them (anthropology), but gives laws *a priori* to them as rational beings. No doubt these laws require a judgment sharpened by experience, in order, on the one hand, to distinguish in what cases they are applicable, and, on the other, to procure for them access to the will of the human being, and effectual influence on conduct; since the human being is acted on by so many inclinations that, though capable of the idea of a practical pure reason, he is not so easily capable of making it effective *in concreto* in his life.

A metaphysics of morals is therefore indispensably necessary, not merely because of a motive of speculation, in order to investigate the sources of the practical principles which are to be found [390] *a priori* in our reason, but also because morals themselves are liable to all sorts of corruption as long as we are without that guide and supreme canon by which to estimate them correctly. For in order that an action should be morally good, it is not enough that it *conform* to the moral law, but it must also be done *for the sake* of the law, otherwise that conformity is only very contingent and uncertain; since a principle which is not moral, although it may now and then produce actions conformable to the law, will also often produce actions which contradict it. Now it is only in a pure philosophy that we can look for the moral law in its purity and genuineness (and, in a practical matter, this is of the utmost consequence): we must, therefore, begin with pure philosophy (metaphysics), and without it there cannot be any moral philosophy at all. That which mingles these pure principles with the empirical does not deserve the name of philosophy (for what distinguishes philosophy from common rational knowledge is that it treats in separate sciences what the latter only comprehends confusedly); much less does it deserve that of moral philosophy, since by this confusion it even spoils the purity of morals themselves and counteracts its own end.

Let it not be thought, however, that what is here demanded already exists in the preparatory study prefixed by the celebrated *Wolff* to his moral philosophy, namely his so-called *universal practical philosophy*,[1] and that, therefore, we have not to strike into an entirely new field. Just because it was to be a general practical philosophy, it has not taken into consideration a will of any particular kind—say, one which should be determined solely from *a priori* principles without any empirical motives, and which we might call a pure will—but volition in general, with all the actions and conditions which belong to it in this general signification. By this it is distinguished from a metaphysics of morals, just as general logic, which treats the acts and canons of pure thought *in general*, is distinguished from transcendental philosophy, which treats of the particular acts and canons of **pure** thought, that is, that whose cognitions are altogether *a priori*. For the metaphysics of morals has to examine the idea and the principles of a possible *pure* will, and not the acts and conditions of human volition generally, which for the most part are drawn from psychology. It is true that moral laws and duty are spoken of in the general practical philosophy (contrary indeed to all fitness). But this is no objection, for in this respect also the authors of that science remain true to their idea of it; they do not distinguish the motives which are prescribed as such by reason alone altogether *a priori*, and which are properly moral, from the empirical motives which the understanding raises to general conceptions merely by comparison of experiences; but without noticing the difference of their sources, and looking on them all as homogeneous, they consider only their greater or less amount. It is in this way they frame their notion of *obligation*, which, though anything but moral, is all that can be asked for in a philosophy which passes no judgment

[391]

---

1 Christian Wolff, *Universal Practical Philosophy* (1738-39).

at all on the *origin* of all possible practical concepts, whether they are *a priori* or only *a posteriori*.[1]

Intending to publish hereafter a metaphysics of morals, I issue in the first instance this groundwork. Indeed there is properly no other foundation for it than the critical examination of a *pure practical reason*;[2] just as that of metaphysics is the critical examination of the pure speculative reason, already published.[3] But in the first place the former is not so absolutely necessary as the latter, because in moral concerns human reason can easily be brought to a high degree of correctness and completeness, even in the commonest understanding, while on the contrary in its theoretic but pure use it is wholly dialectical; and in the second place, if the critique of pure practical reason is to be complete, it must be possible at the same time to show its identity with speculative reason in a common principle, for it can ultimately be only one and the same reason which has to be distinguished merely in its application. I could not, however, bring it to such completeness here without introducing considerations of a wholly different kind, which would be perplexing to the reader. On this account I have adopted the title of *Groundwork for the Metaphysics of Morals* instead of that of *Critique of Pure Practical Reason*.

But in the third place, since a metaphysics of morals, in spite of the discouraging title, is yet capable of being presented in a popular form, and one adapted to the common understanding, I find it useful to separate from it this preliminary treatise on its foundation, in order that I may afterward have no need to intro- [392] duce these necessarily subtle discussions into a book of a more simple character.

The present groundwork is, however, nothing more than the investigation and establishment of *the supreme principle of morality*, and this alone constitutes a study complete in itself, and one which ought to be kept apart from every other moral investigation. No doubt, my conclusions on this weighty question, which has until now been very unsatisfactorily examined, would receive much light from the application of the same principle to the

---

1   Concepts are *a posteriori* in origin if they are derived from specific observations or experiences—including experiences of feelings, inclinations, or impulses.
2   See Kant, *Critique of Practical Reason* (1788). See Appendix B for excerpts.
3   See Kant, *Critique of Pure Reason* (1781, 1787).

whole system, and would be greatly confirmed by the adequacy which it exhibits throughout; but I must forgo this advantage, which indeed would be after all more gratifying than useful, since the easy applicability of a principle and its apparent adequacy give no very certain proof of its soundness, but rather inspire a certain partiality, which prevents us from examining and estimating it strictly in itself, and without regard to its consequences.

I have adopted in this work the method which I think most suitable, proceeding analytically from common knowledge to the determination of its ultimate principle, and again descending synthetically from the examination of this principle and its sources to the common knowledge in which we find it employed. The division will, therefore, be as follows:

1. *First section:* Transition from the common rational moral cognition to the philosophical.

2. *Second section:* Transition from popular moral philosophy to the metaphysics of morals.

3. *Third section:* Final step from the metaphysics of morals to the critique of pure practical reason.

Transition from the Common Rational Moral Cognition to the Philosophical Moral Cognition

Nothing can possibly be conceived in the world, or even out of it, which can be called good without qualification, except a *good will*. Intelligence, wit, judgment, and the other *talents* of the mind, however they may be named, or courage, resolution, perseverance, as qualities of *temperament*, are undoubtedly good and desirable in many respects; but these gifts of nature may also become extremely bad and mischievous if the will which is to make use of them, and which, therefore, constitutes what is called *character*, is not good. It is the same with the *gifts of fortune*. Power, riches, honor, even health, and the general well-being and contentment with one's condition which is called *happiness*, inspire pride, and often presumption, if there is not a good will to correct the influence of these on the mind, and with this also to rectify the whole principle of acting, and adapt it to its end. The sight of a being who is not adorned with a single feature of a pure and good will, enjoying unbroken prosperity, can never give pleasure to an impartial spectator. Thus a good will appears to constitute the indispensable condition even of being worthy of happiness.[1]

There are even some qualities which are of service to this good will itself, and may facilitate its action, yet which have no inner unconditional value, but always presuppose a good will, and this [394] qualifies the esteem that we justly have for them, and does not permit us to regard them as absolutely good. Moderation in the affections and passions, self-control, and calm deliberation are not only good in many respects, but even seem to constitute part of the *inner* worth of the person; but they are far from deserving to be called good without qualification, although they have been so unconditionally praised by the ancients. For without the principles of a good will, they may become extremely evil; and the coldness of a villain not only makes him far more dangerous, but also directly makes him more abominable in our eyes than he would have been without it.

A good will is good not because of what it accomplishes or effects, not by its aptness for the attainment of some proposed end, but simply by virtue of the volition—that is, it is good in

---

1 For more on the worthiness to be happy, see Appendices B and C.

itself, and considered by itself is to be esteemed much higher than all that can be brought about by it in favor of any inclination, or even the sum total of all inclinations. Even if it should happen that, owing to a step-motherly nature, this will should wholly lack power to accomplish its purpose, if with its greatest efforts it should yet achieve nothing, and there should remain only the good will (not, to be sure, a mere wish, but the summoning of all means in our power), then, like a jewel, it would still shine by its own light, as a thing which has its whole value in itself. Its usefulness or fruitlessness can neither add to nor take away anything from this value. It would be, as it were, only the setting to enable us to handle it more conveniently in common commerce, or to attract to it the attention of those who are not yet connoisseurs, but not to recommend it to true connoisseurs, or to determine its value.

There is, however, something so strange in this idea of the absolute value of a mere will, in which no account is taken of its utility, that notwithstanding the thorough assent of even common reason to the idea, yet a suspicion must arise that it may perhaps really be the product of mere high-flown fancy, and that we may [395] have misunderstood the purpose of nature in assigning reason as the governor of our will. Therefore we will examine this idea from this point of view.

In the natural constitution of an organized being, that is, a being adapted suitably to the purposes of life, we assume it as a fundamental principle that no organ for any purpose will be found but what is also the fittest and best adapted for that purpose. Now in a being which has reason and a will, if the proper object of nature were its *preservation*, its *welfare*, in a word, its *happiness*, then nature would have hit upon a very bad arrangement in selecting the reason of the creature to carry out this purpose. For all the actions which the creature has to perform with a view to this purpose, and the whole rule of its conduct, would be far more surely prescribed to it by instinct, and that end would have been attained thereby much more certainly than it ever can be by reason. Should reason have been imparted to this favored creature over and above, it must only have served it to contemplate the happy constitution of its nature, to admire it, to congratulate itself on it, and to feel thankful for it to the beneficent cause, but not that it should subject its desires to that weak and delusive guidance, and meddle incompetently with the purpose of nature. In a word, nature would have taken care that reason should not break forth into *practical use*, nor have the presumption, with its weak insight, to think out for itself the plan of happiness and of the means of attaining it. Nature would not only have taken on herself the choice of the ends but also of the means, and with wise foresight would have entrusted both to instinct.

And, in fact, we find that the more a cultivated reason applies itself with deliberate purpose to the enjoyment of life and happiness, so much more does one fall short of true satisfaction. And from this circumstance there arises in many, if they are candid enough to confess it, a certain degree of *misology*, that is, hatred of reason, especially in the case of those who are most experienced in the use of it, because after calculating all the advantages they derive—I do not say from the invention of all the arts of common luxury, but even from the sciences (which seem to them to be after all only a luxury of the understanding)—they find that they have, in fact, only brought more trouble on their shoulders [396] rather than gained in happiness; and they end by envying rather than despising the more common run of human beings who keep closer to the guidance of mere instinct, and do not allow their reason much influence on their conduct. And this we must admit, that the judgment of those who would very much lower the lofty eulogies of the advantages which reason gives us in regard to the happiness and satisfaction of life, or who would even reduce them below zero, is by no means morose or ungrateful to the goodness with which the world is governed, but that there lies at the root of these judgments the idea that our existence has a different and far worthier end, to which, and not to happiness, is reason's proper vocation, and which must, therefore, be regarded as the supreme condition to which private ends of human beings must, for the most part, defer.

For as reason is not competent to guide the will with certainty in regard to its objects and the satisfaction of all our needs (which it to some extent even multiplies), this being an end to which an implanted instinct would have led with much greater certainty; and since, nevertheless, reason is imparted to us as a practical faculty, that is, as one which is to have influence on the *will*, therefore admitting that nature generally in the distribution of her capacities has adapted the means to the end, its true vocation must be to produce a *will*, not merely good as a *means* to something else, but *good in itself*, for which reason was absolutely necessary. This will then, though not indeed the sole and complete good, must be the supreme good and the condition of every other, even of the desire of happiness. Under these circumstances, there is nothing inconsistent with the wisdom of nature in the fact that the cultivation of reason, which is requisite for the first and unconditioned purpose, does in many ways interfere, at least in this life, with the attainment of the second, which is always conditional—namely, happiness. Indeed, it may even reduce it to nothing, without nature thereby failing of her purpose. For reason recognizes the establishment of a good will as its highest practical vocation, and in attaining this purpose is capable only of a satisfaction of its own proper kind, namely, that from the attainment of an end, which in turn is determined by reason only, notwithstanding that this may involve many a disappointment to the ends of inclination.

[397]   We have then to develop the concept of a will which deserves to be highly esteemed for itself, and is good without a view to anything further, a concept which exists already in the sound natural understanding, requiring rather to be clarified than to be taught, and which in estimating the value of our actions always takes the first place and constitutes the condition of all the rest. In order to do this, we will take the concept of duty, which includes that of a good will, although implying certain subjective limitations and hindrances. These, however, far from concealing it or rendering it unrecognizable, rather bring it out by contrast and make it shine forth so much the brighter.[1]

I omit here all actions which are already recognized as contrary to duty, although they may be useful for this or that purpose, for with these the question whether they are done *from duty* cannot arise at all, since they even conflict with it. I also set aside those actions which really conform to duty, but to which men have *no* immediate *inclination*, performing them because they are impelled thereto by some other inclination. For in this case we can readily distinguish whether the action which agrees with duty is done

---

1 In the following paragraphs, Kant distinguishes among, and provides examples of, three ways agents can be motivated to act rightly. His goal is to clarify the concept of acting from duty. Kant first disregards the usefulness of considering the motivation of an agent to do an act that is wrong. He then discusses motivation (a) from self-love (embodied by the merchant), dismissing it for clearly not exemplifying action from duty. Finally, he distinguishes between acts done (b) from immediate inclination (e.g., preserving one's life from love of life, helping others from uncultivated feelings of sympathy) and acts done (c) from duty (e.g., preserving one's life from duty, helping others when one is circumstantially or temperamentally not emotionally inclined to do so). See the Introduction for discussions of acting from duty and Kant's view of emotions' value and role in morality.

from duty or from a selfish purpose. It is much harder to make this distinction when the action accords with duty, and the subject has besides an *immediate* inclination to it. For example, it is always a matter of duty that a dealer should not overcharge an inexperienced purchaser; and wherever there is much commerce the prudent tradesman does not overcharge, but keeps a fixed price for everyone, so that a child buys from him as well as any other. People are thus *honestly* served; but this is not enough to make us believe that the tradesman has so acted from duty and from principles of honesty; his own advantage required it; it is unwarranted in this case to suppose that he might besides have an immediate inclination in favor of the buyers, so that, as it were, from love he should give no advantage to one over another. Accordingly the action was done neither from duty nor from immediate inclination, but merely with a selfish purpose.

On the other hand, it is a duty to preserve one's life; and, in addition, everyone has also an immediate inclination to do so. But on this account the often anxious care which most people take for it has no intrinsic worth, and their maxim has no moral content. They preserve their life *in conformity with duty*, no doubt, [398] but not *from duty*. On the other hand, if adversity and hopeless sorrow have completely taken away the relish for life, if the unfortunate one, strong in mind, indignant to his fate rather than desponding or dejected, wishes for death, and yet preserves his life without loving it—not from inclination or fear, but from duty—then his maxim has moral content.

To be beneficent when one can is a duty; and besides this, there are many minds so sympathetically constituted that, without any other motive of vanity or self-interest, they find a pleasure in spreading joy around them, and can take delight in the satisfaction of others so far as it is their own work. But I maintain that in such a case an action of this kind, however proper, however amiable it may be, has nevertheless no true moral worth, but is on a level with other inclinations, for example, the inclination to honor, which if it is happily directed to that which is in fact of public utility and accordant with duty, and consequently honorable, deserves praise and encouragement, but not esteem. For the maxim lacks the moral content, namely, that such actions be done *from duty*, not from inclination. Put the case that the mind of that philanthropist was clouded by sorrow of his own, extinguishing all sympathy with the lot of others, and that while he still has the power to benefit others in distress, he is not touched by their trouble because he is absorbed with his own; and now suppose that he tears himself out of this dead insensibility and performs the action without any inclination to it, but simply from duty, then for the first time his action has its genuine moral worth. Further still, if nature has put little sympathy in the heart of this or that man, if he, supposed to be an upright man, is by temperament cold and indifferent to the sufferings of others, perhaps because in respect of his own he is provided with the special gifts of patience and fortitude, and supposes, or even requires, that others should have the same—and such a man would certainly not be the meanest product of nature—but if nature had not specially framed him for a philanthropist, would he not still find in himself a source from which to give himself a far higher worth than that of a good-natured temperament could be? Unquestionably. It is just in this that the moral worth of the character is brought out which is incomparably the highest of all, namely, that he is beneficent, not from inclination, but from duty.[1]

[399]

To secure one's own happiness is a duty, at least indirectly; for discontent with one's condition, under a pressure of many anxieties and amidst unsatisfied needs, might easily become a great *temptation to transgression of duty*. But here again, without looking to duty, all men have already the strongest and most intimate inclination to happiness, because it is just in this idea that all inclinations are combined in one total. But the precept of happiness is often of such a sort that it greatly interferes with some inclinations, and yet a human being cannot form any definite and certain conception of the sum of satisfaction of all of them which is called happiness. It is not then to be wondered at that a single inclination, definite both as to what it promises and as to the time within which it can be gratified, is often able to overcome such a fluctuating idea, and that a gouty patient, for instance, can choose to enjoy what he likes, and to suffer what he may, since, according to his calculation, on this occasion at least, he has not sacrificed the enjoyment of the present moment to a possibly mistaken expectation of a happiness which is supposed to be found in health. But even in this case, if the general inclination to happiness did not influence his will, and supposing that in his particular case health was not a necessary element in this calculation, there yet remains in this, as in all other cases, this law—namely,

---

1 See Appendix G for Schiller on acting from duty; and Appendix E for Kant's discussion of sympathy as a duty in the *Metaphysics of Morals*, "Doctrine of Virtue."

that he should promote his happiness not from inclination but from duty, and by this would his conduct first acquire true moral worth.[1]

It is in this manner, undoubtedly, that we are to understand those passages of Scripture also in which we are commanded to love our neighbor, even our enemy. For love, as an inclination, cannot be commanded, but beneficence for duty's sake may, even though we are not impelled to it by any inclination—indeed, are even repelled by a natural and unconquerable aversion. This is *practical* love, and not *pathological*—a love which is seated in the will, and not in the propensities of feeling—in principles of action and not of tender sympathy; and it is this love alone which can be commanded.

The second[2] proposition is: That an action done from duty derives its moral worth, *not from the purpose* which is to be attained by it, but from the maxim by which it is determined, and therefore does not depend on the realization of the object of the action, but merely on the *principle of volition* by which the action has taken place, without regard to any object of desire. It is clear from what precedes that the purposes which we may have in view in our action, or their effects regarded as ends and incentives of the will, cannot give to actions any unconditional or moral worth. In what, then, can their worth lie if it is not to consist in the will in reference to its expected effect? It cannot lie anywhere but in the *principle of the will* without regard to the ends which can be attained by the action. For the will stands between its *a priori* principle, which is formal, and its *a posteriori* incentive, which is material, as between two roads, and as it must be determined by something, it follows that it must be determined by the formal principle of volition when an action is done from duty, in which case every material principle has been withdrawn from it. [400]

The third proposition, which is a consequence of the two preceding, I would express thus: *Duty is the necessity of acting from respect for the law.* I may have *inclination* for an object as the effect of my proposed action, but *never respect* for it, just because it is an effect and not an activity of will. Similarly, I cannot have respect

---

1 In this paragraph, Kant compares (a) inclination-based yet prudent pursuit of one's own happiness with (b) impulsive, imprudent pursuit of immediate pleasure, and (c) duty-based pursuit of one's own happiness (as an indirect duty).

2 [The first proposition was that to have moral worth an action must be done from duty.]

for inclination, whether my own or another's; I can at most, if my own, approve it; if another's, sometimes even love it, that is, look on it as favorable to my own interest. It is only what is connected with my will as a principle, by no means as an effect—what does not serve my inclination, but outweighs it, or at least in case of choice excludes it from its calculation—in other words, simply the law of itself, which can be an object of respect, and hence a command. Now an action done from duty must wholly exclude the influence of inclination, and with it every object of the will, so that nothing remains which can determine the will except objectively the *law*, and subjectively *pure respect* for this practical law, [401] and consequently the maxim[1] that I should follow this law even to the thwarting of all my inclinations.

Thus the moral worth of an action does not lie in the effect expected from it, nor in any principle of action which needs to borrow its motive from this expected effect. For all these effects—agreeableness of one's condition, and even the promotion of the happiness of others—could have been also brought about by other causes, so that for this there would have been no need of the will of a rational being; whereas it is in this alone that the supreme and unconditional good can be found. The pre-eminent good which we call moral can therefore consist in nothing else than *the representation of the law* in itself, *which certainly is only possible in a rational being*, insofar as this representation, and not the expected effect, determines the will. This is a good which is already present in the person who acts accordingly, and we need not wait for it to appear first in the result.[2]

---

1 A *maxim* is the subjective principle of volition. The objective principle (i.e., that which would also serve subjectively as a practical principle to all rational beings if reason had full power over the faculty of desire) is the practical *law*. [I.K.]

2 It might be here objected to me that I take refuge behind the word *respect* in an obscure feeling, instead of giving a distinct solution of the question by a concept of reason. But although respect is a feeling, it is not a feeling *received* through influence, but is *self-wrought* by a rational concept, and, therefore, is specifically distinct from all feelings of the former kind, which may be referred either to inclination or fear. What I recognize immediately as a law for me, I recognize with respect. This merely signifies the consciousness that my will is *subordinate* to a law, without the intervention of other influences on my sense. The immediate determination of the will by the law, and the consciousness of this, is called respect, so that this is regarded as an *effect* of the law on the subject, and not as the *cause* of it. Respect is properly the conception of a worth that

But what sort of law can that be, the conception of which must [402] determine the will, even without paying any regard to the effect experienced from it, in order that this will may be called good absolutely and without qualification? As I have deprived the will of every impulse which could arise for it from obedience to any particular law, there remains nothing but the universal conformity of its actions to law in general, which alone is to serve the will as a principle, that is, I am never to act otherwise than so *that I could also will that my maxim should become a universal law.*[1] Here, now, it is the simple lawfulness in general, without assuming any particular law applicable to certain actions, that serves the will as its principle, and must so serve it if duty is not to be a vain delusion and a chimerical notion. The common reason of human beings in its practical judgments perfectly coincides with this, and always has in view the principle here suggested.

Let the question be, for example: May I when in distress make a promise with the intention not to keep it? I readily distinguish here between the two significations which the question may have: whether it is prudent or whether it is right to make such a false promise. The former may undoubtedly often be the case. I see clearly indeed that it is not enough to extricate myself from a present difficulty by means of this subterfuge, but it must be well considered whether there may not hereafter spring from this lie much greater inconvenience than that from which I now seek to free myself, and as, with all my supposed *cunning*, the consequences cannot be so easily foreseen but that credit once lost may be much more injurious to me than any mischief which I seek to avoid at present, it should be considered whether it would not be *more prudent* to act herein according to a universal maxim, and to

---

thwarts my self-love. Accordingly it is something which is considered neither an object of inclination nor of fear, although it has something analogous to both. The *object* of respect is the *law* only, that is, the law that we impose on *ourselves*, and yet recognize as necessary in itself. As a law, we are subjected to it without consulting self-love; as imposed by us on ourselves, it is a result of our will. In the former aspect it has an analogy to fear, in the latter to inclination. Respect for a person is properly only respect for the law (of honesty, etc.) of which he gives us an example. Since we also see in a person of talents, as it were, the *example of the law* (viz. to become like him in this by exercise), and this constitutes our respect. All so-called moral *interest* consists simply in *respect* for the law. [I.K.]

1 This is the first appearance of what Kant will call, in the next section, the "categorical imperative."

make it a habit to promise nothing except with the intention of keeping it. But it is soon clear to me that such a maxim will still only be based on the fear of consequences. Now it is a wholly different thing to be truthful from duty than to be so from apprehension of injurious consequences. In the first case, the very notion of the action already implies a law for me; in the second case, I must first look about elsewhere to see what results may be combined with it which would affect myself. For to deviate from the principle of duty is beyond all doubt evil; but to be unfaithful to my maxim of prudence may often be very advantageous to me, although to abide by it is certainly safer. The shortest way, however, and an unerring one, to discover the answer to this question whether a lying promise is consistent with duty, is to ask myself: Would I be content that my maxim (to extricate myself from difficulty by a false promise) should hold as a universal law, for myself as well as for others? And would I be able to say to myself, "Everyone may make a deceitful promise when he finds himself in a difficulty from which he cannot otherwise extricate himself"? Then I presently become aware that, while I can will the lie, I can by no means will that lying become a universal law. For with such a law there would be no promises at all, since it would be in vain to profess my intention in regard to my future actions to those who would not believe this profession, or if they over-hastily did so, would pay me back in my own coin. Hence my maxim, as soon as it should be made a universal law, would necessarily destroy itself.

[403]

I do not, therefore, need any far-reaching penetration to discern what I have to do in order that my volition may be morally good. Inexperienced in the course of the world, incapable of being prepared for all its contingencies, I only ask myself: Can you also will that your maxim should be a universal law? If not, then it must be rejected, and that not because of a disadvantage accruing from it to myself or even to others, but because it cannot enter as a principle into a possible universal legislation, and reason extorts from me immediate respect for such legislation. I do not indeed as yet *discern* on what this respect is based (this the philosopher may inquire), but at least I understand this—that it is an estimation of the worth which far outweighs all worth of what is recommended by inclination, and that the necessity of acting from *pure* respect for the practical law is what constitutes duty, to which every other motive must give place because it is the condition of a will that is good *in itself*, and the worth of such a will is above everything.

Thus, then, without quitting the moral cognition of common human reason, we have arrived at its principle. And although, no doubt, common human reason does not conceive it in such an abstract and universal form, yet it really always has it before its eyes and uses it as the standard of judgment. Here it would be [404] easy to show how, with this compass in hand, common human reason is well able to distinguish, in every case that occurs, what is good, what evil, conformable to duty or inconsistent with it, if, without in the least teaching it anything new, we only, like Socrates, direct its attention to the principle it itself employs; and that, therefore, we do not need science and philosophy to know what we should do to be honest and good, yes, even to be wise and virtuous. Indeed we might well have conjectured beforehand that the acquaintance with what every human being is obligated to do, and therefore also to know, would be within the reach of every human being, even the commonest. Here we cannot with-hold admiration when we see how great an advantage practical judgment has over the theoretical in the common human understanding. In the latter, if common reason ventures to depart from the laws of experience and from the perceptions of the senses, it falls into mere inconceivabilities and self-contradictions, at least into a chaos of uncertainty, obscurity, and instability. But in the practical sphere it is just when the common understanding excludes all sensible incentives from practical laws that its power of judgment begins to show itself to advantage. It then becomes even subtle, whether it be that it quibbles with its own conscience or with other claims regarding what is to be called right, or whether it desires for its own instruction to determine honestly the worth of its actions; and, in the latter case, it may even have as good a hope of hitting the mark as any philosopher whatever can promise himself. Indeed it is almost more sure of doing so, because the philosopher cannot have any other principle, while he may easily perplex his judgment by a multitude of considerations foreign to the matter, and so turn aside from the right way. Would it not therefore be wiser in moral concerns to acquiesce in the judgment of common reason, or at most only to call in philosophy for the purpose of rendering the system of morals more complete and intelligible, and its rules more convenient for use (especially disputation), but not so as to draw off the common understanding from its happy simplicity, or bring it by means of philosophy into a new path of inquiry and instruction?

Innocence is indeed a glorious thing; but, on the other hand, it is very sad that it cannot well maintain itself, and is easily [405] seduced. On this account even wisdom—which otherwise consists more in conduct than in knowledge—still has need of science, not in order to learn from it, but to secure for its precepts admission and permanence. Against all the commands of duty which reason represents to the human being as so deserving of respect, he feels in himself a powerful counterweight in his needs and inclinations, the entire satisfaction of which he sums up under the name of happiness. Now reason issues commands unyieldingly, without promising anything to the inclinations, and, as it were, with disregard and contempt for these claims, which are so impetuous and at the same time so plausible, and which will not allow themselves to be suppressed by any command. Hence there arises a *natural dialectic*, that is, a disposition to argue against these strict laws of duty and to question their validity, or at least their purity and strictness; and if possible, to make them more compatible with our wishes and inclinations, that is to say, to corrupt them at their very source and entirely destroy their worth—a thing which even common practical reason cannot ultimately approve.

Thus is the *common human reason* compelled to go out of its sphere and to take a step into the field of *practical philosophy*, not to satisfy any speculative need (which never occurs to it as long as it is content to be mere sound reason), but rather on practical grounds, in order to attain in it information and clear instruction respecting the source of its principle, and the correct determination of it in opposition to the maxims which are based on wants and inclinations, so that it may escape from the perplexity of opposite claims, and not run the risk of losing all genuine moral principles through the equivocation into which it easily falls. Thus, when practical reason cultivates itself, there insensibly arises in it a dialectic which forces it to seek aid in philosophy, just as happens to it in its theoretical use; and in this case, therefore, as well as in the other, it will find rest nowhere but in a thorough critical examination of our reason.

Transition from Popular Moral Philosophy to the Metaphysics of Morals

If we have so far drawn our notion of duty from the common use of our practical reason, it is by no means to be inferred that we have treated it as an empirical concept. On the contrary, if we attend to the experience of human conduct, we meet frequent and, as we ourselves allow, just complaints that one cannot find a single, certain example of the disposition to act from pure duty. Although many things are done *in conformity with* what *duty* prescribes, it is nevertheless always doubtful whether they are done strictly *from duty*, and so have moral worth. Hence there have at all times been philosophers who have altogether denied that this disposition actually exists at all in human actions, and have ascribed everything to a more or less refined self-love. Not that they have on that account questioned the soundness of the conception of morality; on the contrary, they spoke with sincere regret of the frailty and impurity of human nature,[1] which, though noble enough to take as its rule an idea so worthy of respect, is yet too weak to follow it; and employs reason, which ought to give it the law, only for the purpose of providing for the interest of the inclinations, whether singly or at the best in the greatest possible harmony with one another.

In fact, it is absolutely impossible to make out by experience [407] with complete certainty a single case in which the maxim of an action, however right in itself, rested simply on moral grounds and on the representation of duty. Sometimes it happens that with the sharpest self-examination we can find nothing beside the moral principle of duty which could have been powerful enough to move us to this or that action and to so great a sacrifice; yet we cannot from this infer with certainty that it was not really some secret impulse of self-love, under the false appearance of duty, that was the actual determining cause of the will. We like then to flatter ourselves by falsely taking credit for a more noble motive;

---

1 Frailty and impurity are the two lesser degrees of radical evil. (The worst is wickedness.) Frailty is the tendency not to live up to the moral maxims one has adopted; impurity is the tendency to rely on (and to need to rely on) non-moral incentives of action in order to act rightly. For more on the radical evil in human nature, see the excerpt from *Religion within the Limits of Reason Alone* in Appendix D.

whereas in fact we can never, even by the strictest examination, get completely behind the secret incentives, since, when the question is of moral worth, it is not with the actions which we see that we are concerned, but with those inward principles of them which we do not see.

Moreover, we cannot better serve the wishes of those who ridicule all morality as mere chimera of human imagination overstepping itself from vanity, than by conceding to them that concepts of duty must be drawn only from experience (as, from indolence, people are ready to think is the case with all other concepts also); for this is to prepare for them a certain triumph. I am willing to admit out of love for humanity that even most of our actions are in conformity with duty; but if we look closer at them we everywhere come upon the dear self which is always prominent; and it is this they have in view, and not the strict command of duty, which would often require self-denial. Without being an enemy of virtue, a cool observer, one that does not mistake the wish for good, however lively, for its reality, may sometimes doubt whether true virtue is actually found anywhere in the world, and this especially as years increase and the judgment is partly made wiser by experience, and partly also more acute in observation. This being so, nothing can secure us from falling away altogether from our ideas of duty, or maintain in the soul a well-grounded respect for its law, but the clear conviction that although there should never have been actions which really sprang from such [408] pure sources, yet whether this or that takes place is not at all the question; but that reason itself, independent of all experience, ordains what ought to take place, that accordingly actions of which perhaps the world has so far never given an example, the feasibility even of which might be very much doubted by one who founds everything on experience, are nevertheless inflexibly commanded by reason; that, for example, even though there might never have been a sincere friend, yet not a whit less is pure sincerity in friendship required of everyone, because, prior to all experience, this duty is involved (as duty in general) in the idea of a reason[1] determining the will by *a priori* principles.

When we add further that, unless we deny that the notion of morality has any truth or reference to any possible object, we must admit that its law must be valid, not merely for human beings, but for all *rational beings as such*, not merely under certain

---

1 An "idea of reason" is a concept not attainable through experience.

contingent conditions or with exceptions, but with *absolute necessity*, then it is clear that no experience could enable us to infer even the possibility of such apodictic[1] laws. For with what right could we bring into unbounded respect as a universal precept for all rational nature that which perhaps holds only under the contingent conditions of humanity? Or how could laws of the determination of *our* will be regarded as laws of the determination of the will of rational beings as such, and for us only as such, if they were merely empirical and did not take their origin wholly *a priori* from pure but practical reason?

Nor could anything be more fatal to morality than that we should wish to derive it from examples. For every example of it that is set before me must first itself be judged by principles of morality, as to whether it is worthy to serve as an original example, that is, as a model; but by no means can it authoritatively furnish the conception of morality. Even the Holy One of the Gospels must first be compared with our ideal of moral perfection before we can recognize Him as such; and so He says of Himself, "Why do you call Me (whom you see) good; none is good (the model of good) but God only (whom you do not see)?"[2] But whence have we the conception of God as the supreme good? Simply from the *idea* of moral perfection, which   [409] reason frames *a priori* and connects inseparably with the notion of a free will. Imitation finds no place at all in morality, and examples serve only for encouragement, that is, they put beyond all doubt the feasibility of what the law commands, they make visible that which the practical rule expresses more generally, but they can never authorize us to set aside the true original which lies in reason, and to guide ourselves by examples.

If there is no genuine supreme principle of morality but what must rest simply on pure reason, independent on all experience, I think it is not necessary even to ask the question whether it is good to exhibit these concepts in their generality (*in abstracto*) as they are established *a priori* along with the principles belonging to them, if our knowledge is to be distinguished from the *common* and to be called philosophical. In our times indeed this might perhaps be necessary; for if we collected votes, whether pure

---

1 "Apodictic" means necessary, and often suggests an epistemological aspect. Kant says that geometrical propositions are all apodictic, meaning that they are "combined with the consciousness of their necessity" (*Critique of Pure Reason*, B41).

2 See Luke 18:19 and Matthew 19:17.

rational knowledge separated from everything empirical, that is to say, a metaphysics of morals, or whether popular practical philosophy is to be preferred, it is easy to guess which side would predominate.[1]

This descending to popular notions is certainly very commendable if the ascent to the principles of pure reason has first taken place and been satisfactorily accomplished. This implies that we first *ground* the doctrine of morals on metaphysics, and then, when it is firmly established, procure *entry* for it by giving it a popular character. But it is quite absurd to try to be popular in the first inquiry, on which the soundness of the principles depends. It is not only that this procedure can never lay claim to the very rare merit of a true *philosophical popularity*, since there is no art in being intelligible if one renounces all thoroughness of insight; but also it produces a disgusting medley of compiled observations and half-reasoned principles. Shallow minds enjoy this because it can be used for everyday chat, but the sagacious find in it only confusion, and being unsatisfied and unable to help themselves, they turn away their eyes, while philosophers, who [410] see quite well through this delusion, are little listened to when they call people off for a time from this pretended popularity in order that they might be rightfully popular after they have attained a definite insight.

We need only to look at the attempts of moralists in that favorite fashion, and we will find at one time the special constitution of human nature (including, however, the idea of a rational nature generally), at one time perfection, at another time happiness, here moral sense, there fear of God, a little of this and a little of that, in marvelous mixture, without its occurring to them to ask whether the principles of morality are to be sought in the knowledge of human nature at all (which we can have only from experience); and, if this is not so—if these principles are to be found altogether *a priori*, free from everything empirical, in pure rational concepts only, and nowhere else, not even in the smallest degree—then rather to adopt the method of making this a separate inquiry, as pure practical philosophy, or (if one may use a

---

1 One of Kant's contemporaries whom he probably considered among the practitioners of "popular practical philosophy" is Christian Garve (1742-98). Kant responds to criticisms Garve raised against his ethics in the excerpt from "On the Common Saying: 'This May Be True in Theory, but It Does Not Apply in Practice,'" Appendix C.

name so decried) as metaphysics[1] of morals, to bring it by itself to completeness, and to require the public, which wishes for popular treatment, to await the outcome of this undertaking.

Such a metaphysics of morals, completely isolated, not mixed with any anthropology, theology, physics, or hyperphysics, and still less with occult qualities (which we might call hypophysical), is not only an indispensable substratum of all sound theoretical knowledge of duties, but is at the same time a desideratum of the highest importance to the actual fulfilment of their precepts. For the pure thought of duty, unmixed with any foreign addition of empirical attractions, and, in a word, the thought of the moral law, exercises on the human heart, by way of reason alone (which first becomes aware with this that it can of itself be practical), an influence so much more powerful than all other incentives[2] which may be derived from the field of experience that in the consciousness of its dignity it despises the latter, and can by degrees become their master; whereas a mixed doctrine of morals, compounded partly of incentives drawn from feelings and inclinations, and partly also of conceptions of reason, must make the

[411]

---

1 Just as pure mathematics is distinguished from applied, and pure logic from applied, so if we choose we may also distinguish pure philosophy of morals (metaphysics) from applied (viz., applied to human nature). By this designation we are also at once reminded that moral principles are not based on properties of human nature, but must be capable of being deduced for every rational nature, and accordingly also for human nature. [I.K.]

2 I have a letter from the late excellent [Johann Georg] Sulzer [(1720-79)], in which he asks me why moral instruction, although containing much that is convincing for reason, yet accomplishes so little. My answer was postponed in order that I might make it complete. But it is simply this, that the teachers themselves have not got their own concepts clear, and when they endeavor to make up for this by raking up motives of moral goodness from every quarter, trying to make their medicine right strong, they spoil it. For the commonest understanding shows that if we imagine, on the one hand, an act of honesty done with steadfast mind, apart from every view to advantage of any kind in this world or another, and even under the greatest temptations of necessity or allurement, and, on the other hand, a similar act which was affected, in however low a degree, by a foreign incentive, the former leaves far behind and eclipses the second; it elevates the soul, and inspires the wish to be able to act in like manner oneself. Even moderately young children feel this impression, and one should never represent duties to them in any other light. [I.K.]

mind waver between motives which cannot be brought under any principle, which lead to good only by mere accident, and very often also to evil.

From what has been said, it is clear that all moral concepts have their seat and origin completely *a priori* in reason, and that, moreover, in the commonest reason just as truly as in that which is in the highest degree speculative; that they cannot be obtained by abstraction from any empirical, and therefore merely contingent, cognitions; that it is just this purity of their origin that makes them worthy to serve as our supreme practical principle, and that just in proportion as we add anything empirical, we detract from their genuine influence and from the absolute value of actions; that it is not only of the greatest necessity, in a purely speculative point of view, but is also of the greatest practical importance, to derive these concepts and laws from pure reason, to present them pure and unmixed, and even to determine the compass of this practical or pure rational cognition, that is, to determine the whole faculty of pure practical reason; and, in [412] doing so, we must not make its principles dependent on the particular nature of human reason, though in speculative philosophy this may be permitted, or may even at times be necessary; but since moral laws ought to hold good for every rational being, we must derive them from the universal concept of a rational being. In this way, although for its *application* to human beings morality has need of anthropology, yet, in the first instance, we must treat it in itself (a thing which in such distinct branches of science is easily done); knowing well that, unless we are in possession of this, it would not only be vain to determine the moral element of duty in right actions for purposes of speculative criticism, but it would be impossible to base morals on their genuine principles, even for common practical purposes, especially for moral instruction, so as to produce pure moral dispositions, and to engraft them on people's minds to the promotion of the greatest possible good in the world.

But in order that in this study we may not merely advance by the natural steps from the common moral judgment (in this case very worthy of respect) to the philosophical, as has been already done, but also from a popular philosophy, which goes no further than it can reach by groping with the help of examples, to metaphysics (which does not allow itself to be checked by anything empirical and, as it must measure the whole extent of this kind of rational knowledge, goes as far as ideal conceptions, where even examples fail us), we must follow and clearly describe the practical faculty of reason, from the general rules of its determination to the point where the concept of duty springs from it.

Everything in nature works according to laws. Rational beings alone have the capacity to act *in accordance with the representation of laws*—that is, according to principles, that is, have a *will*. Since the deduction of actions from principles requires *reason*, the will is nothing but practical reason. If reason infallibly determines the will, then the actions of such a being which are recognized as objectively necessary are subjectively necessary also, that is, the will is a capacity to choose *that only* which reason independent of inclination recognizes as practically necessary, that is, as good. But if reason of itself does not sufficiently determine the will, if the latter is subject also to subjective conditions (particular incentives) which do not always coincide with the objective conditions, in a word, if the will does not *in itself* completely accord with reason (which is actually the case with human beings), then the actions which objectively are recognized as necessary are subjectively contingent, and the determination of such a will according to objective laws is *necessitation*, that is to say, the relation of the objective laws to a will that is not thoroughly good is conceived as the determination of the will of a rational being by principles of reason, but which the will from its nature does not necessarily follow. [413]

The conception of an objective principle, in so far as it is obligatory for a will, is called a command (of reason), and the formula of the command is called an **imperative**.

All imperatives are expressed through an *ought*, and thereby indicate the relation of an objective law of reason to a will which from its subjective constitution is not necessarily determined by it (a necessitation). They say that something would be good to do or to forbear, but they say it to a will which does not always do a thing because it is represented to be good to do it. That is *practically good*, however, which determines the will by means of the representations of reason, and consequently not from subjective causes, but objectively, that is, on principles which are valid for every rational being as such. It is distinguished from the agreeable as that which influences the will only by means of feeling from merely subjective causes, valid only for the senses of this or that one, and not as a principle of reason which holds for everyone.[1]

A perfectly good will would therefore be equally subject to objective laws (viz. laws of good), but could not be conceived as *necessitated* thereby to act lawfully, because of itself from its subjective constitution it can only be determined by the conception of good. Therefore no imperatives hold for the Divine will, or in general for a *holy* will; *ought* is here out of place because the volition is already of itself necessarily in unison with the law. Therefore imperatives are only formulae to express the relation of objective laws of all volition to the subjective imperfection of the will of this or that rational being, for example, a human will.

Now all imperatives command either *hypothetically* or *categorically*. The former represent the practical necessity of a possible action as means to something else that is willed (or at least which one might possibly will). The categorical imperative would be that which represented an action as necessary of itself without reference to another end, that is, as objectively necessary.

Since every practical law represents a possible action as good, and on this account, for a subject who is practically determinable by reason, as necessary, all imperatives are formulae determining an action which is necessary according to the principle of a will good in some respects. If now the action is good only as a means *to something else*, then the imperative is *hypothetical*; if it is conceived as good *in itself* and consequently as being necessarily the principle of a will which of itself conforms to reason, then it is *categorical*.

---

1 The dependence of the faculty of desire on sensations is called inclination, and this accordingly always indicates a *need*. The dependence of a contingently determinable will on principles of reason is called an *interest*. This, therefore, is found only in the case of a dependent will which does not always of itself conform to reason; in the Divine will we cannot conceive any interest. But the human will can also *take an interest* in a thing without therefore acting *from interest*. The former signifies the *practical* interest in the action, the latter the *pathological* interest in the object of the action. The former indicates only dependence on principles of reason for the sake of inclination, reason supplying only the practical rules how the requirement of the inclination may be satisfied. In the first case the action interests me; in the second the object of the action (because it is pleasant to me). We have seen in the first section that in an action done from duty we must look not to the interest in the object, but only to that in the action itself, and in its rational principle (viz., the law). [I.K.]

Thus the imperative declares what action possible by me would be good, and presents the practical rule in relation to a will which does not forthwith perform an action simply because it is good, whether because the subject does not always know that it is good, or because, even if it know this, yet its maxims might be opposed to the objective principles of practical reason.

Accordingly the hypothetical imperative only says that the action is good for some purpose, *possible* or *actual*. In the first case, it is a **problematic**, in the second an **assertoric**, practical principle. The categorical imperative which declares an action to be objectively necessary in itself without reference to any purpose, without any other end, is valid as an **apodictic** (practical) principle. [415]

Whatever is possible only by the power of some rational being may also be conceived as a possible purpose of some will; and therefore the principles of action as regards the means necessary to attain some possible purpose are in fact infinitely numerous. All sciences have a practical part consisting of problems expressing that some end is possible for us, and of imperatives directing how it may be attained. These may, therefore, be called in general imperatives of **skill**. Here there is no question whether the end is rational and good, but only what one must do in order to attain it. The precepts for the physician to make his patient thoroughly healthy, and for a poisoner to ensure certain death, are of equal value in this respect, that each serves to effect its purpose perfectly. Since in early youth it cannot be known what ends are likely to occur to us in the course of life, parents seek to have their children taught a *great many things*, and provide for their *skill* in the use of means for all sorts of *discretionary* ends, of none of which can they determine whether it may not perhaps hereafter be an object to their pupil, but which it is at all events *possible* that he might aim at; and this anxiety is so great that they commonly neglect to form and correct their children's judgment of the value of the things which may be chosen as ends.

There is *one* end, however, which may be assumed to be actually such to all rational beings (so far as imperatives apply to them, viz. as dependent beings), and therefore, one purpose which they not merely *may* have, but which we may with certainty assume that they all actually *do have* by a natural necessity, and this is *happiness*. The hypothetical imperative which expresses the practical necessity of an action as means to the advancement of happiness is *assertoric*. We are not to present it as necessary for an uncertain and merely possible purpose, but for a purpose which we may presuppose with certainty and *a priori* [416] in every human being, because it belongs to his being. Now skill in the choice of means to his own greatest well-being may be called *prudence*,[1] in the narrowest sense. And thus the imperative which refers to the choice of means to one's own happiness, that is, the precept of prudence, is still always *hypothetical*; the action is not commanded absolutely, but only as means to another purpose.

Finally, there is an imperative which commands a certain conduct immediately, without having as its condition any other purpose to be attained by it. This imperative is **categorical**. It concerns not the matter of the action, or its intended result, but its form and the principle of which it is itself a result; and what is essentially good in it consists in the mental disposition, let the consequence be what it may. This imperative may be called that of **morality**.

There is a marked distinction also between the volitions on these three sorts of principles in the *dissimilarity* of the necessitation of the will. In order to mark this difference more clearly, I think they would be most suitably named in their order if we said they are either *rules* of skill, or *counsels* of prudence, or *commands* (*laws*) of morality. For it is law only that involves the concept of an *unconditional* and objective necessity, which is consequently universally valid; and commands are laws which must be obeyed, that is, must be followed, even in opposition to inclination. *Counsels*, indeed, involve necessity, but one which can only hold under a contingent subjective condition, viz., they depend on whether this or that human being counts this or that as part of his happiness; the categorical imperative, on the contrary, is not limited by any condition, and as being absolutely, although practically, necessary may be quite properly called a command. We might also call the first kind of imperatives *technical* (belonging to art), the

---

1 The word *prudence* is taken in two senses: in the one it may bear the name of knowledge of the world, in the other that of private prudence. The former is a human being's ability to influence others so as to use them for his own purposes. The latter is the sagacity to combine all these purposes for his own lasting benefit. This latter is properly that to which the value even of the former is reduced, and when someone is prudent in the former sense but not in the latter, we might better say of him that he is clever and cunning, but, on the whole, imprudent. [I.K.]

second *pragmatic*[1] (belonging to welfare), and the third *moral* [417]
(belonging to free conduct as such, that is, to morals).

Now arises the questions, how are all these imperatives possible? This question does not seek to know how we can conceive the performance of the action which the imperative ordains, but merely how we can conceive the necessitation of the will which the imperative expresses. No special explanation is needed to show how an imperative of skill is possible. Whoever wills the end wills also (so far as reason has decisive influence on his action) the means in his power which are indispensably necessary to it. This proposition is, as regards the volition, analytic; for in willing an object as my effect there is already thought the causality of myself as an acting cause, that is to say, the use of the means; and the imperative educes from the concept of a volition of an end the concept of actions necessary to this end. Synthetic propositions must no doubt be employed in defining the means to a proposed end; but they do not concern the principle, the act of the will, but the object and its realization.[2] For example, that in order to bisect a line on an unerring principle I must draw from its extremities two intersecting arcs; this no doubt is taught by mathematics only in synthetic propositions; but if I know that it is only by this process that the intended operation can be performed, then to say that if I fully will the operation, I also will the action required for it, is an analytic proposition; for it is one and the same thing to represent something as an effect which I can produce in a certain way, and to represent myself as acting in this way.

If it were only equally easy to give a definite conception of happiness, the imperatives of prudence would correspond exactly with those of skill, and would likewise be analytic. For in this case as in that, it could be said whoever wills the end wills also (nec-

---

1 It seems to me that the proper signification of the word *pragmatic* may be most accurately defined this way. For *sanctions* are called pragmatic which flow properly, not from the law of the states as necessary enactments, but from *precaution* for the general welfare. A history is composed pragmatically when it teaches *prudence*, that is, instructs the world how it can provide for its interests better, or at least as well as the human beings of former time. [I.K.]
2 As Kant here implies, analytic propositions state a subject-predicate relationship in which the predicate is already contained in the thought of the subject, and (at most) needs to be drawn out through analysis; synthetic propositions add something new to the subject—something not already contained in its concept.

essarily in accordance with reason) the indispensable means
thereto which are in his power. But, unfortunately, the notion of
happiness is so indeterminate that although every human being
wishes to attain it, yet he never can say definitely and consistently what it is that he really wishes and wills. The reason for this is
that all the elements which belong to the concept of happiness are
altogether empirical, that is, they must be borrowed from experience, and nevertheless the idea of happiness requires an absolute
whole, a maximum of welfare in my present and all future circumstances. Now it is impossible that the most clear-sighted and
at the same time most powerful being (supposed finite) should
frame for himself a definite conception of what he really wills in
this. If he wills riches, how much anxiety, envy, and snares might
he not thereby draw upon his shoulders? If he wills knowledge
and discernment, perhaps it might prove to be only an eye so
much sharper to show him so much the more fearfully the evils
that are now concealed from him and that cannot be avoided, or
to impose more wants on his desires, which already give him concern enough. Would he have long life? Who guarantees to him that
it would not be a long misery? Would he at least have health? How
often has uneasiness of the body restrained from excesses into
which perfect health would have allowed one to fall, and so on?
In short, he is unable, on any principle, to determine with certainty what would make him truly happy; because to do so he
would need to be omniscient. We cannot therefore act on any definite principles to secure happiness, but only on empirical counsels, for example, of regimen, frugality, courtesy, reserve, etc.,
which experience teaches do, on the average, most promote well-
being. Hence it follows that the imperatives of prudence do not,
strictly speaking, command at all, that is, they cannot present
actions objectively as practically *necessary*; that they are rather to
be regarded as counsels (*consilia*) than precepts (*praecepta*) of reason, that the problem to determine certainly and universally what
action would promote the happiness of a rational being is completely insoluble, and consequently no imperative respecting it is
possible which would, in the strict sense, command him to do
what makes him happy; because happiness is not an ideal of reason but of imagination, resting solely on empirical grounds, and
it is vain to expect that these should determine an action by which
one could attain the totality of a series of consequences which is
really endless. This imperative of prudence would, however, be an
analytic proposition if we assume that the means to happiness
could be certainly assigned; for it is distinguished from the imper-

ative of skill only by this, that in the latter the end is merely *possible*, in the former it is *given*; as, however, both only ordain the means to that which we suppose to be willed as an end, it follows that the imperative which ordains the willing of the means to him who wills the end is in both cases analytic. Thus there is no difficulty in regard to the possibility of an imperative of this kind either.

On the other hand, the question, how the imperative of *morality* is possible, is undoubtedly one, the only one, demanding a solution, as this is not at all hypothetical, and the objective necessity which it presents cannot rest on any hypothesis, as is the case with the hypothetical imperatives. Only here we must never leave out of consideration that we *cannot* make out *by means of any example*, in other words, empirically, whether there is such an imperative at all; but it is rather to be feared that all those which seem to be categorical may yet be at bottom hypothetical. For instance, when the precept is: "You ought not to promise deceitfully," and it is assumed that the necessity of this is not a mere counsel to avoid some other ill, so that it should mean: "You shall not make a lying promise, lest if it become known you should destroy your credit," but that an action of this kind must be regarded as evil in itself, so that the imperative of the prohibition is categorical; then we cannot show with certainty in any example that the will was determined merely by the law, without any other incentives, although it may appear to be so. For it is always possible that fear of disgrace, perhaps also obscure dread of other dangers, may have a secret influence on the will. Who can prove by experience the non-existence of a cause when all that experience tells us is that we do not perceive it? But in such a case the so-called moral imperative, which as such appears to be categorical and unconditional, would in reality be only a pragmatic precept, drawing our attention to our own interests, and merely teaching us to take these into consideration.

We will therefore have to investigate *a priori* the possibility of a *categorical* imperative, as we have not in this case the advantage of [420] its reality being given in experience, so that [the elucidation of] its possibility should be requisite only for its explanation, not for its establishment. In the meantime it may be discerned beforehand that the categorical imperative alone has the purport of a practical law; and the rest may indeed be called *principles* of the will but not laws, since whatever is only necessary for the attainment of some discretionary purpose may be considered as in itself contingent, and we can at any time be free from the precept if we give up the purpose; on the contrary, the unconditional command leaves the will no liberty to choose the opposite, consequently it alone carries with it that necessity which we require of a law.

Secondly, in the case of this categorical imperative or law of morality, the difficulty (of describing its possibility) is a very profound one. It is an *a priori* synthetic practical proposition;[1] and as there is so much difficulty in discerning the possibility of speculative propositions of this kind, it may readily be supposed that the difficulty will be no less with the practical.

In this problem we will first inquire whether the mere concept of a categorical imperative may not perhaps supply us also with the formula of it, containing the proposition which alone can be a categorical imperative; for even if we know the tenor of such an absolute command, yet how it is possible will require further special and laborious study, which we postpone to the last section.[2]

When I conceive a hypothetical imperative, in general I do not know beforehand what it will contain until I am given the condition. But when I conceive a categorical imperative, I know at once what it contains. For as the imperative contains besides the law only the necessity that the maxims[3] shall conform to this law, while the law contains no conditions restricting it, there remains nothing but the general statement that the maxim of the action should conform to universal law, and it is this conformity alone that the imperative properly represents as necessary.

[421]

---

1 I connect the act with the will without presupposing any condition resulting from any inclination, but *a priori*, and therefore necessarily (though only objectively, that is, assuming the idea of a reason possessing full power over all subjective motives). This is accordingly a practical proposition which does not deduce the willing of an action by mere analysis from another already presupposed (for we have not such a perfect will), but connects it immediately with the conception of the will of a rational being, as something not contained in it. [I.K.]

2 Kant now shifts his focus to the content of a categorical imperative, suspending the discussion of how a categorical imperative is possible.

3 A *maxim* is a subjective principle of action, and must be distinguished from the *objective principle*, namely, the practical law. The former contains the practical rule set by reason according to the conditions of the subject (often its ignorance or its inclinations), so that it is the principle on which the subject acts; but the law is the objective principle valid for every rational being, and is the principle on which it *ought to act*—that is, an imperative. [I.K.]

There is therefore but one categorical imperative, namely, this: *Act only on that maxim whereby you can at the same time will that it become a universal law.*[1]

Now if all imperatives of duty can be deduced from this one imperative as their principle, then, although it should remain undecided whether what is called duty is not merely a vain notion, yet at least we shall be able to show what we understand by it and what this notion means.

Since the universality of the law according to which effects are produced constitutes what is properly called *nature* in the most general sense (as to form)—that is, the existence of things so far as it is determined by general laws—the imperative of duty may be expressed thus: *Act as if the maxim of your action were to become by your will a **universal law of nature**.*

We will now enumerate a few duties, adopting the usual division of them into duties to ourselves and duties to others, and into perfect and imperfect duties.[2]

1. Someone reduced to despair by a series of misfortunes feels wearied of life, but is still so far in possession of his reason that [422] he can ask himself whether it would not be contrary to his duty to himself take his own life. Now he inquires whether the maxim of his action could become a universal law of nature. His maxim is: From self-love I adopt it as my principle to shorten my life when its longer duration is likely to bring more ill than satisfaction. It is asked then simply whether this principle founded on self-love can become a universal law of nature. Now we can see at once that a system of nature of which it should be a law to destroy life by means of the very feeling whose vocation it is to impel to the improvement of life would contradict itself, and therefore

---

1 This formulation of the categorical imperative, the "formula of universal law" (along with its variant, the "formula of the law of nature") has been a primary target for criticism. For two related criticisms, see Fichte in Appendix F and Hegel in Appendix H.

2 It must be noted here that I reserve the division of duties for a future *metaphysics of morals;* so that I give it here only as an arbitrary one (in order to arrange my examples). For the rest, I understand by a perfect duty one that admits no exception in favor of inclination, and then I have not merely external but also internal perfect duties. This is contrary to the use of the word adopted in the schools; but I do not intend to justify it here, as it is all one for my purpose whether it is admitted or not. [I.K.] On Kant's division of duties, see the Introduction and Appendix E.

could not exist as a system of nature; hence that maxim cannot possibly exist as a universal law of nature, and consequently would be wholly inconsistent with the supreme principle of all duty.

2. Another finds himself forced by necessity to borrow money. He knows that he will not be able to repay it, but sees also that nothing will be lent to him unless he promises firmly to repay it within in a determinate time. He wants to make this promise, but he has still so much conscience as to ask himself: Is it not unlawful and inconsistent with duty to get out of a difficulty this way? Suppose, however, that he resolves to do so, then the maxim of his action would be expressed thus: When I think myself in want of money, I will borrow money and promise to repay it, although I know that I never can do so. Now this principle of self-love or of one's own advantage may perhaps be consistent with my whole future welfare; but the question now is, Is it right? I change then the suggestion of self-love into a universal law, and state the question thus: How would it be if my maxim were a universal law? Then I see at once that it could never hold as a universal law of nature, but would necessarily contradict itself. For supposing it to be a universal law that everyone when he thinks himself in a difficulty should be able to promise whatever he pleases, with the purpose of not keeping his promise, the promise itself would become impossible, as well as the end that he might have in view in it, since no one would consider that anything was promised to him, but would ridicule all such statements as vain pretenses.

3. A third finds in himself a talent which with the help of some culture might make him a useful human being in many [423] respects. But he finds himself in comfortable circumstances and prefers to indulge in pleasure rather than to take pain in enlarging and improving his fortunate natural predispositions. He asks, however, whether his maxim of neglect of his natural gifts, besides agreeing with his inclination to indulgence, agrees also with what is called duty. He sees then that a system of nature could indeed subsist with such a universal law, although human beings (like the South Sea islanders) should let their talents rust and resolve to devote their lives merely to idleness, amusement, and propagation of their species—in a word, to enjoyment; but he cannot possibly **will** that this should be a universal law of nature, or be implanted in us as such by a natural instinct. For as a rational being, he necessarily wills that his faculties be developed, since they serve him, and have been given him, for all sorts of purposes.

4. Yet a fourth, who is in prosperity, while he sees that others have to contend with great wretchedness and that he could help them, thinks: What concern is it of mine? Let everyone be as happy as heaven pleases, or as he can make himself; I will take nothing from him nor even envy him, only I do not wish to contribute anything to his welfare or to his assistance in need! Now no doubt, if such a mode of thinking were a universal law, the human race might very well subsist, and doubtless even better than in a state in which everyone talks of sympathy and good-will, or even takes care occasionally to put it into practice, but, on the other side, also cheats when he can, betrays the rights of human beings, or otherwise violates them. But although it is possible that a universal law of nature might exist in accordance with that maxim, it is impossible to **will** that such a principle should have the universal validity of a law of nature. For a will which resolved this would contradict itself, inasmuch as many cases might occur in which one would have need of the love and sympathy of others, and in which, by such a law of nature, sprung from his own will, he would deprive himself of all hope of the aid he desires.

These are a few of the many actual duties, or at least what we regard as such, which obviously fall into two classes on the one principle that we have laid down. We must *be able to will* that a [424] maxim of our action should be a universal law. This is the canon of the moral judgment of the action generally. Some actions are of such a character that their maxim cannot without contradiction be even *conceived* as a universal law of nature, far from it being possible that we should *will* that it *should* be so. In others, this intrinsic impossibility is not found, but still it is impossible to *will* that their maxim should be raised to the universality of a law of nature, since such a will would contradict itself. It is easily seen that the former violate strict or rigorous (inflexible) duty; the latter only wide (meritorious) duty. Thus it has been completely shown by these examples how all duties depend as regards the nature of the obligation (not the object of the action) on the same principle.

If now we attend to ourselves on occasion of any transgression of duty, we will find that we in fact do not will that our maxim should be a universal law, for that is impossible for us; on the contrary, we will that the opposite should remain a universal law, only we assume the liberty of making an *exception* in our own favor or (just for this time only) in favor of our inclination. Consequently, if we considered all cases from one and the same point of view, namely, that of reason, we should find a contradiction in our own will, namely, that a certain principle should be objectively necessary as a universal law, and yet subjectively should not be universal, but admit of exceptions. As, however, we at one moment regard our action from the point of view of a will wholly conformed to reason, and then again look at the same action from the point of view of a will affected by inclination, there is not really any contradiction, but an opposition (*antagonismus*) of inclination to the precept of reason, whereby the universality (*universalitas*) of the principle is changed into a mere generality (*generalitas*), so that the practical principle of reason shall meet the maxim half way. Now, although this cannot be justified in our own impartial judgment, yet it proves that we do really recognize the validity of the categorical imperative and (with all respect for it) only allow ourselves a few exceptions which we think unimportant and forced upon us.

[425]   We have thus established at least this much—that if duty is a conception which is to have any import and real legislative authority for our actions, it can only be expressed in categorical, and not at all in hypothetical, imperatives. We have also, which is of great importance, exhibited clearly and definitely for every practical application the content of the categorical imperative, which must contain the principle of all duty if there is such a thing at all. We have not yet, however, advanced so far as to prove *a priori* that there actually is such an imperative, that there is a practical law which commands absolutely of itself and without any other incentive, and that the following of this law is duty.

With the view of attaining to this it is of extreme importance to remember that we must not allow ourselves to think of deducing the reality of this principle from the *particular attributes of human nature*. For duty is to be a practical, unconditional necessity of action; it must therefore hold for all rational beings (to whom an imperative can apply at all), and *for this reason only* be also a law for all human wills. On the contrary, whatever is deduced from the particular natural characteristics of humanity, from certain feelings and propensities, or even, if possible, from any particular tendency proper to human reason, and which need not necessarily hold for the will of every rational being—this may indeed supply us with a maxim but not with a law; with a subjective principle on which we may have a propensity and inclination to act, but not with an objective principle on which we should be *enjoined* to act, even though all our propensities, inclinations, and natural dispositions were opposed to it. In fact, the sublimity and intrinsic dignity of the command in duty are so much the more evident, the less the subjective impulses favor it and the more they oppose it, without being able in the slightest degree to weaken the obligation of the law or to diminish its validity.

Here then we see philosophy brought to a critical position, since it has to be firmly fixed, notwithstanding that it has nothing to support it in heaven or on earth. Here it must show its purity as absolute director of its own laws, not the herald of those which are whispered to it by an implanted sense or who knows what tutelary nature. Although these may be better than nothing, yet they can never afford principles dictated by reason, which must [426] have their source wholly *a priori* and, at the same time, their commanding authority from this, expecting everything from the supremacy of the law and the due respect for it, nothing from inclination, or else condemning the human being to self-contempt and inward abhorrence.

Thus every empirical element is not only quite incapable of being an aid to the principle of morality, but is even highly prejudicial to the purity of morals; for the proper and inestimable worth of an absolutely good will consists just in this, that the principle of action is free from all influence of contingent grounds, which alone experience can furnish. We cannot too much or too often repeat our warning against this lax and even mean habit of thought which seeks for its principle among empirical motives and laws; for human reason in its weariness is glad to rest on this pillow, and in a dream of sweet illusions (in which, instead of Juno, it embraces a cloud) it substitutes for morality a bastard patched up from limbs of various derivation, which looks like anything one chooses to see in it; only not like virtue to one who has once beheld her in her true form.[1]

The question then is this: Is it a necessary law *for all rational beings* that they should always judge their actions by maxims of which they can themselves will that they should serve as universal laws? If there is such a law, then it must be connected (altogether *a priori*) with the very concept of the will of a rational being as such. But in order to discover this connection we must, however reluctantly, take a step into metaphysics, although into a [427]

---

1 To behold virtue in her proper form is nothing else but to contemplate morality stripped of all admixture of sensible things and of every spurious ornament of reward or self-love. How much she then eclipses everything else that appears charming to the affections, every one may readily perceive with the least exertion of his reason, if his reason is not wholly spoiled for abstraction. [I.K.]

domain of it which is distinct from speculative philosophy—namely, the metaphysics of morals. In a practical philosophy, where it is not the grounds of what *happens* that we have to ascertain, but the laws of what *ought to happen*, even though it never does, that is, objective practical laws, there it is not necessary to inquire into the grounds why anything pleases or displeases, how the pleasure of mere sensation differs from taste, and whether the latter is distinct from a general satisfaction of reason; on what the feeling of pleasure or pain rests, and how from it desires and inclinations arise, and from these again maxims by the cooperation of reason; for all this belongs to an empirical psychology, which would constitute the second part of the doctrine of nature, if we regard physics as the *philosophy of nature*, so far as it is based *on empirical laws*. But here we are concerned with objective practical laws, and consequently with the relation of the will to itself so far as it is determined by reason alone, in which case whatever has reference to anything empirical is necessarily excluded; since if *reason of itself alone* determines the conduct (and it is the possibility of this that we are now investigating), it must necessarily do so *a priori*.

The will is conceived as a capacity of determining itself to action in accordance with the *representation of certain laws*. And such a capacity can be found only in rational beings. Now that which serves the will as the objective ground of its self-determination is the *end*, and if this is assigned by reason alone, it must hold for all rational beings. On the other hand, that which merely contains the ground of possibility of the action of which the effect is the end, this is called the *means*. The subjective ground of the desire is the *incentive*, the objective ground of the volition is the *motive*; hence the distinction between subjective ends which rest on incentives, and objective ends which depend on motives valid for every rational being. Practical principles are *formal* when [428] they abstract from all subjective ends; they are *material* when they assume these, and therefore particular incentives. The ends which a rational being proposes to himself at pleasure as *effects* of his actions (material ends) are all only relative, for it is only their relation to the particular desires of the subject that gives them their worth, which therefore cannot furnish principles universal and necessary for all rational beings and for every volition, that is to say, practical laws. Hence all these relative ends can give rise only to hypothetical imperatives.

Supposing, however, that there were something *whose existence* has *in itself* an absolute worth, something which, being *an end in itself,* could be a source of definite laws, then in this and this alone would lie the source of a possible categorical imperative, that is, a practical law.

Now I say: the human being and in general every rational being exists as an end in itself, *not merely as a means* to be arbitrarily used by this or that will, but in all his actions, whether they concern himself or other rational beings, must be always regarded at the same time as an end. All objects of the inclinations have only a conditional worth; for if the inclinations and the needs founded on them did not exist, then their object would be without any value. But the inclinations themselves, being sources of needs, are so far from having an absolute worth for which they should be desired that, on the contrary, it must be the universal wish of every rational being to be wholly free from them. Thus the worth of any object which is *to be acquired* by our action is always conditional. Beings whose existence depends not on our will but on nature's, have nevertheless, if they are nonrational beings, only a relative value as means, and are therefore called *things;* rational beings, on the contrary, are called *persons,* because their very nature restricts all choice (and is an object of respect).[1] These, therefore, are not merely subjective ends whose existence has a worth *for us* as an effect of our action, but *objective ends,* that is, things whose existence is an end in itself—an end, moreover, for which no other can be substituted, to which they should serve *merely* as means, for otherwise nothing whatever would possess *absolute worth;* but if all worth were conditioned and therefore contingent, then there would be no supreme practical principle of reason whatever.

If then there is a supreme practical principle or, with respect to the human will, a categorical imperative, it must be one which, being drawn from the conception of that which is necessarily an end for everyone because it is *an end in itself,* constitutes an *objective* principle of will, and can therefore serve as a universal practical law. The foundation of this principle is: *rational nature exists as an end in itself.* The human being necessarily conceives of his [429] own existence as being so; so far then this is a *subjective* principle of human actions. But every other rational being regards its exis-

---

1 This passage makes explicit Kant's view that nonrational animals lack the dignity that Kant attributes to persons, and thus cannot be owed respect or consequent duties. For Kant's account of our duties regarding animals, and his rationale for them, see Appendix E, *Metaphysics of Morals,* 6:433.

tence similarly, just on the same rational principle that holds for me;[1] so that it is at the same time an objective principle from which as a supreme practical law all laws of the will must be capable of being deduced. Accordingly the practical imperative will be as follows: *So act as to treat humanity, whether in your own person or in that of any other, in every case at the same time as an end, never as a means only.*[2] We will now inquire whether this can be practically carried out.

To abide by the previous examples:

First, under the head of necessary duty to oneself: Someone who contemplates suicide should ask himself whether his action can be consistent with the idea of humanity *as an end in itself.* If he destroys himself in order to escape from painful circumstances, he uses a person merely as a *means* to maintain a tolerable condition up to the end of life. But a human being is not a thing, that is to say, something which can be used merely as a means, but must in all his actions be always considered as an end in itself. I cannot, therefore, dispose in any way of a human being in my own person by mutilating, damaging, or killing him. (It belongs to morals proper to define this principle more precisely, so as to avoid all misunderstanding, for example, as to the amputation of the limbs in order to preserve myself; as to exposing my life to danger with a view to preserve it, etc. This question is therefore omitted here.)[3]

Second, as regards necessary duties, or those of strict obligation, towards others: He who is thinking of making a lying promise to others will see at once that he would be using another human being *merely as a means*, without the latter at the same time containing in himself the end. For he whom I propose by [430] such a promise to use for my own purposes cannot possibly assent to my mode of acting toward him, and therefore cannot himself contain the end of this action. This violation of the principle of humanity in other human beings is more obvious if we

---

1 This proposition is here stated as a postulate. The ground of it will be found in the concluding section. [I.K.]

2 This formulation, the "formula of humanity," is criticized by Fichte in Appendix F. Note the similarities between this formulation and the "supreme principle of the doctrine of virtue" in Appendix E, *Metaphysics of Morals*, 6:395. The latter principle also contains traces of the formula of universal law.

3 See *Metaphysics of Morals*, 6:422-44, in Appendix E for Kant's promised, fuller exposition of this duty.

take in examples of attacks on the freedom and property of others. For then it is clear that he who transgresses the rights of human beings intends to use the person of others merely as means, without considering that as rational beings they ought always to be esteemed also as ends, that is, as beings who must be capable of containing in themselves the end of the very same action.[1]

Third, as regards contingent (meritorious) duties to oneself: It is not enough that the action does not violate humanity in our own person as an end in itself, it must also *harmonize with* it. Now there are in humanity capacities of greater perfection which belong to the end that nature has in view with regard to humanity in ourselves as the subject; to neglect these might perhaps be consistent with the *maintenance* of humanity as an end in itself, but not with the *advancement* of this end.

Fourth, as regards meritorious duties toward others: The natural end which all human beings have is their own happiness. Now humanity might indeed subsist although no one should contribute anything to the happiness of others, provided he did not intentionally withdraw anything from it; but after all, this would only harmonize negatively, not positively, with *humanity as an end in itself,* if everyone does not also endeavor, as far as he can, to forward the ends of others. For the ends of any subject which is an end in itself ought as far as possible to be *my* ends also, if that conception is to have its *full* effect in me.

This principle that humanity and generally every rational nature is *an end in itself* (which is the supreme limiting condition of every human being's freedom of action), is not borrowed from experience, *first,* because it is universal, applying as it does to all rational beings whatever, and experience is not capable of determining anything about them; *second,* because it does not present humanity as an end to human beings (subjectively), that is, as an [431]

---

1 Let it not be thought that the common: *quod tibi non vis fieri, etc.,* [i.e., what you do not want others to do to you, do not do to them] could serve here as the rule or principle. For it is only a deduction from the former, though with several limitations; it cannot be a universal law, for it does not contain the principle of duties to oneself, nor of the duties of benevolence to others (for many a one would gladly consent that others should not benefit him, provided only that he might be excused from showing benevolence to them), nor finally that of duties of strict obligation to one another, for on this principle the criminal might argue against the judge who punishes him, and so on. [I.K.]

object which human beings do of themselves actually adopt as an end; but as an objective end which must as a law constitute the supreme limiting condition of all our subjective ends, let them be what they will; it must therefore spring from pure reason. In fact the ground of all practical legislation lies (according to the first principle) *objectively in the rule* and its form of universality which makes it capable of being a law (say, for example, a law of nature); but *subjectively* in the *end*; now by the second principle, the subject of all ends is each rational being inasmuch as it is an end in itself. From this follows the third practical principle of the will, which is the ultimate condition of its harmony with the universal practical reason, viz., the idea of *the will of every rational being as a will giving universal law.*[1]

On this principle all maxims are rejected which are inconsistent with the will being itself universal legislator. Thus the will is not merely subject to the law, but subject to it so that it must be regarded *as itself giving the law*, and on this ground only subject to the law (of which it can regard itself as the author).

In the previous imperatives, namely, that based on the conception of the conformity of actions to general laws, as in a *system of nature*, and that based on the universal *prerogative* of rational beings as *ends* in themselves—these imperatives just because they were conceived as categorical excluded from any share in their authority all admixture of any interest as an incentive; they were, however, only *assumed* to be categorical, because such an assumption was necessary to explain the conception of duty. But we could not prove independently that there are practical propositions which command categorically, nor can it be proved in this section; one thing, however, could be done, namely, to indicate in the imperative itself, by some determinate expression, that in the case of volition from duty all interest is renounced, which is the specific criterion of categorical as distinguished from hypothetical imperatives. This is done in the present third formula of the principle, namely, in the idea of the will of every rational being as a *will giving universal law.*

[432]

For although a will *which is subject to laws* may be attached to this law by means of an interest, yet a will which is itself a supreme lawgiver, so far as it is such, cannot possibly depend on any interest, since a will so dependent would itself still need another law restricting the interest of its self-love by the condition that it should be valid as universal law.

---

1 This is called the "formula of autonomy."

Thus the *principle* of every human will as *a will which in all its maxims gives universal laws*,[1] provided it be otherwise correct, would be very *well suited* to be the categorical imperative in this respect, namely, that just because of the idea of universal legislation it is *not based on any interest*, and therefore it alone among all possible imperatives can be *unconditional*. Or still better, converting the proposition, if there is a categorical imperative (that is, a law for the will of every rational being), it can only command that everything be done from maxims of one's will regarded as a will which could at the same time will that it should itself give universal laws, for in that case only the practical principle and the imperative which it obeys are unconditional, since they cannot be based on any interest.

Looking back now on all previous attempts to discover the principle of morality, we need not wonder why they all failed. It was seen that the human being is bound to laws by duty, but it was not observed that the laws to which he is subject are *only those of his own giving*, though at the same time they are *universal*, and that he is only bound to act in conformity with his own will—a will, however, which is designed by nature to give universal laws. For when one has conceived the human being only as subject to a law (no matter what), then this law required some interest, [433] either by way of attraction or constraint, since it did not originate as a law from *his own* will, but this will was according to a law obliged by *something else* to act in a certain manner. Now by this necessary consequence all the labor spent in finding a supreme principle of *duty* was irrevocably lost. For one never elicited duty, but only a necessity of acting from a certain interest. Whether this interest was private or otherwise, in any case the imperative had to be conditional, and could not by any means be capable of being a moral command. I will therefore call this the principle of **autonomy** of the will, in contrast with every other which I accordingly count under **heteronomy**.

The concept of every rational being as one which must consider itself as giving in all the maxims of its will universal laws, so as to judge itself and its actions from this point of view—this concept leads to another which depends on it and is very fruitful, namely, that of a *kingdom of ends*.

---

1 I may be excused from adducing examples to elucidate this principle, as those which have already been used to elucidate the categorical imperative and its formula would all serve the like purpose here. [I.K.]

By a *kingdom* I understand the systematic union of different rational beings through common laws. Now since it is by laws that the universal validity of ends are determined, hence, if we abstract from the personal differences of rational beings, and likewise from all the content of their private ends, we shall be able to conceive all ends combined in a systematic whole (including both rational beings as ends in themselves, and also the special ends which each may propose to himself), that is to say, we can conceive a kingdom of ends, which on the preceding principles is possible.

For all rational beings come under the *law* that each of them must treat itself and all others *never merely as means*, but in every case *at the same time as ends in themselves*. From this results a systematic union of rational beings through common objective laws, that is, a kingdom which may be called a kingdom of ends, since what these laws have in view is just the relation of these beings to one another as ends and means. It is certainly only an ideal.

A rational being belongs as a *member* to the kingdom of ends when, although giving universal laws in it, he is also himself subject to these laws. He belongs to it *as sovereign* when, while giving laws, he is not subject to the will of any other.

[434] A rational being must always regard himself as giving laws either as member or as sovereign in a kingdom of ends which is rendered possible by the freedom of will. He cannot, however, maintain the latter position merely by maxims of his will, but only in case he is a completely independent being without needs and with unrestricted power adequate to his will.

Morality consists then in the reference of all action to the legislation which alone can render a kingdom of ends possible. This legislation must be capable of existing in every rational being, and of emanating from his will, so that the principle of this will is never to act on any maxim which could not without contradiction be also a universal law, and accordingly always so to act that *the will could at the same time regard itself as giving through its maxims universal laws*. If now the maxims of rational beings are not by their own nature coincident with this objective principle, then the necessity of acting on it is called practical necessitation, that is, *duty*. Duty does not apply to the sovereign in the kingdom of ends, but it does apply to every member of it and to all in the same degree.

The practical necessity of acting on this principle, that is, duty, does not rest at all on feelings, impulses, or inclinations, but solely on the relation of rational beings to one another, a relation in which the will of a rational being must always be regarded as *legislative*, since otherwise it could not be regarded as *an end in itself*. Reason then refers every maxim of the will, regarding it as legislative universally, to every other will and also to every action towards oneself; and this not on account of any other practical motive or any future advantage, but from the idea of the *dignity* of a rational being, obeying no law but that which he himself also gives.

In the kingdom of ends everything has either *price* or *dignity*. Whatever has price can be replaced by something else which is *equivalent*; whatever, on the other hand, is above all price, and therefore admits of no equivalent, has a dignity.

Whatever has reference to the general inclinations and wants of humankind has a *market price*; whatever, without presupposing a need, corresponds to a certain taste, that is, to a delight in the mere purposeless play of our faculties, has a *fancy price*; but that which constitutes the condition under which alone anything can be an end in itself, this has not merely relative worth, that is, price, but an inner worth, that is, *dignity*.   [435]

Now morality is the condition under which alone a rational being can be an end in himself, since by this alone it is possible that he should be a legislating member in the kingdom of ends. Thus morality, and humanity, insofar as it is capable of morality, is that which alone has dignity. Skill and diligence in labor have a market price; wit, lively imagination, and humor have a fancy price; on the other hand, fidelity to promises, benevolence from principle (not from instinct), have an inner worth. Neither nature nor art contains anything which in default of these it could put in their place, for their worth consists not in the effects which spring from them, not in the use and advantage which they secure, but in the disposition, that is, the maxims of the will which are ready to manifest themselves in such actions, even if they do not have the desired effect. These actions also need no recommendation from any subjective taste or sentiment, that they may be looked upon with immediate favor and delight; they need no immediate propensity or feeling for them; they exhibit the will that performs them as an object of an immediate respect, and nothing but reason is required to *impose* them on the will; not to *flatter* it into them, which, in the case of duties, would be a contradiction. This estimation therefore shows that the worth of such a disposition is dignity, and places it infinitely above all price, with which it cannot for a moment be brought into comparison or competition without as it were violating its sanctity.

What then is it which justifies virtue or the morally good disposition, in making such lofty claims? It is nothing less than the *privilege* it secures to the rational being of participating *in the giving of universal laws,* by which it qualifies him to be a member of a possible kingdom of ends, a privilege to which he was already destined by his own nature as being an end in itself, and on that account legislating in the kingdom of ends; free as regards all laws of nature, and obeying only those laws which he himself gives, and by which his maxims can belong to a system of universal law [436] to which at the same time he submits himself. For nothing has any worth except what the law assigns it. Now the legislation itself which assigns the worth of everything must for that very reason possess dignity, that is, an unconditional incomparable worth; and the word *respect* alone supplies a becoming expression for the esteem which a rational being must have for it. *Autonomy* then is the basis of the dignity of human nature and of every rational nature.

The three modes of presenting the principle of morality that have been adduced are at bottom only so many formulae of the very same law, and each unites in itself the other two. There is, however, a difference among them, but it is subjectively rather than objectively practical, intended, namely, to bring an idea of reason nearer to intuition (by means of a certain analogy), and thereby nearer to feeling. All maxims, in fact, have—

1. A *form,* consisting in universality; and in this view the formula of the moral imperative is expressed thus, that the maxims must be so chosen as if they were to serve as universal laws of nature.

2. A *matter,* namely, an end, and here the formula says that the rational being, as it is an end by its own nature and therefore an end in itself, must in every maxim serve as the condition limiting all merely relative and arbitrary ends.

3. A *complete determination* of all maxims by means of that formula, namely, that all maxims ought, by their own legislation, to harmonize with a possible kingdom of ends as with a kingdom of nature.[1] There is a progression here in the order of the categories

---

1 Teleology considers nature as a kingdom of ends; ethics regards a possible kingdom of ends as a kingdom of nature. In the first case, the kingdom of ends is a theoretical idea, adopted to explain what actually is. In the latter it is a practical idea, adopted to bring about that which is not yet, but which can be realized by our conduct, namely, if it conforms to this idea. [I.K.]

of *unity* of the form of the will (its universality), *plurality* of the matter (the objects, that is, the ends), and *totality* of the system of these. In forming our moral *judgment* of actions it is better to proceed always on the strict method, and start from the universal formula of the categorical imperative: *Act according to a maxim which* [437] *can at the same time make itself a universal law.* If, however, we wish to gain an *entrance* for the moral law, it is very useful to bring one and the same action under the three specified conceptions, and thereby as far as possible to bring it nearer to intuition.

We can now end where we started at the beginning, namely, with the conception of a will unconditionally good. *That will is absolutely good* which cannot be evil—in other words, whose maxim, if made a universal law, could never contradict itself. This principle, then, is its supreme law: *Act always on such a maxim as you can at the same time will to be a universal law*; this is the sole condition under which a will can never contradict itself; and such an imperative is categorical. Since the validity of the will as a universal law for possible actions is analogous to the universal connection of the existence of things by universal laws, which is the formal notion of nature in general, the categorical imperative can also be expressed thus: *Act on maxims which can at the same time have for their object themselves as universal laws of nature.* Such then is the formula of an absolutely good will.

Rational nature is distinguished from the rest of nature by this, that it sets before itself an end. This end would be the matter of every good will. But since in the idea of a will that is absolutely good without being limited by any condition (of attaining this or that end) we must abstract wholly from every end *to be effected* (since this would make every will only relatively good), it follows that in this case the end must be conceived, not as an end to be effected, but as an *independently existing* end. Consequently it is conceived only negatively, that is, as that which we must never act against, and which, therefore, must never be regarded merely as a means, but must in every volition be esteemed also as an end. Now this end can be nothing but the subject of all possible ends, since this is also the subject of a possible absolutely good will; for such a will cannot without contradiction be subordinated to any other object. This principle: So act in regard to every rational being (yourself and others) that he may always have a place in your maxim as an end in itself, is accordingly essentially identical with this other: Act upon a maxim which, at the same time, con- [438] tains in itself its own universal validity for every rational being. For that in using means for every end I should limit my maxim by the condition of its holding good as a law for every subject, this comes to the same thing as that the fundamental principle of all maxims of action must be that the subject of all ends, that is, the rational being himself, be never employed merely as a means, but as the supreme condition restricting the use of all means—that is, in every case also as an end.

It follows incontestably that, to whatever laws any rational being may be subject, he (being an end in itself) must be able to regard himself as also legislating universally in respect to these same laws, since it is just this fitness of his maxims for universal legislation that distinguishes him as an end in itself; also it follows that this implies his dignity (prerogative) above all merely natural beings, that he must always take his maxims from the point of view which regards himself, and likewise every other rational being, as a lawgiving being (on which account they are called persons). In this way a world of rational beings (*mundus intelligibilis*) is possible as a kingdom of ends, and this by virtue of the legislation proper to all persons as members. Therefore, every rational being must so act as if he were by his maxims in every case a legislating member in the universal kingdom of ends. The formal principle of these maxims is: So act as if your maxim were to serve also as the universal law (of all rational beings). A kingdom of ends is thus only possible on the analogy of a kingdom of nature, the former, however, only by maxims—that is, self-imposed rules—the latter only by the laws of efficient causes acting under necessitation from without. Nevertheless, although the system of nature is looked upon as a machine, yet so far as it has reference to rational beings as its ends, it is given on this account the name of a kingdom of nature. Now such a kingdom of ends would be actually realized by means of maxims conforming to the canon which the categorical imperative prescribes to all rational beings, *if they were universally followed*. But although a rational being, even if he strictly follows this maxim himself, cannot count on all others being therefore true to the same, nor expect the kingdom of nature and its orderly arrangements to be in harmony with him as a fitting member, so as to form a kingdom of ends to which he himself contributes, that is to say, that it shall favor his expectation of happiness, still that law: Act according to the maxims of a member of a merely possible kingdom of ends legislating in it universally,[1] remains in its full force inasmuch as it commands cate-

[439]

---

1 This is called the "formula of the kingdom of ends."

gorically. And it is just in this that the paradox lies, that the mere dignity of the human being as a rational being, without any other end or advantage to be attained thereby, in other words, respect for a mere idea, should yet serve as an inflexible precept of the will, and that it is precisely in this independence of the maxim on all such incentives that its sublimity consists; and it is this that makes every rational subject worthy to be a legislative member in the kingdom of ends, for otherwise he would have to be conceived only as subject to the natural law of his needs. And although we should suppose the kingdom of nature and the kingdom of ends to be unified under one sovereign, so that the latter kingdom thereby ceased to be a mere idea and acquired true reality, then it would no doubt gain the addition of a strong incentive, but by no means any increase in its inner worth. For this sole absolute lawgiver must, notwithstanding this, be always thought as estimating the worth of rational beings only by their own disinterested behavior, as prescribed to themselves from that idea alone. The essence of things is not altered by their external relations, and that which, abstracting from these, alone constitutes the absolute worth of a human being is also that by which he must be judged, whoever the judge may be, and even by the Supreme Being. *Morality*, then, is the relation of actions to the autonomy of the will, that is, to the potential universal legislation by its maxims. An action that is consistent with the autonomy of the will is *permitted*; one that does not agree with it is *forbidden*. A will whose maxims necessarily coincide with the laws of autonomy is a *holy* will, good absolutely. The dependence of a will not absolutely good on the principle of autonomy (moral necessitation) is obligation. This, then, cannot be applied to a holy being. The objective necessity of actions from obligation is called *duty*.

From what has just been said, it is easy to see how it happens that, although the conception of duty implies subjection to the law, we yet ascribe a certain *dignity* and sublimity to the person [440] who fulfills all his duties. There is not, indeed, any sublimity in him, so far as he is *subject* to the moral law; but inasmuch as in regard to that very law he is likewise a *legislator*, and on that account alone subject to it, he has sublimity. We have also shown above that neither fear nor inclination, but simply respect for the law, is the incentive which can give actions a moral worth. Our own will, so far as we suppose it to act only under the condition that its maxims are potentially universal laws, this ideal will which is possible for us is the proper object of respect; and the dignity of humanity consists just in this capacity of being universally legislative, though with the condition that it is itself subject to this same legislation.

The Autonomy of the Will as the Supreme Principle of Morality

Autonomy of the will is that property of it by which it is a law unto itself (independently of any property of the objects of volition). The principle of autonomy then is this: Always to choose so that the maxims of the choice are contained in the same volition as a universal law. We cannot prove that this practical rule is an imperative, that is, that the will of every rational being is necessarily bound to it as a condition, by a mere analysis of the concepts which occur in it, since it is a synthetic proposition; we must advance beyond the cognition of the objects to a critical examination of the subject, that is, pure practical reason, for this synthetic proposition which commands apodictically must be capable of being cognized wholly *a priori*. This matter, however, does not belong to the present section. But that the principle of autonomy in question is the sole principle of morals can be readily shown by mere analysis of the concepts of morality. For by this analysis we find that its principle must be a categorical imperative, and that what this commands is neither more nor less than this very autonomy.

[441] ## Heteronomy of the Will as the Source of All Spurious Principles of Morality

If the will seeks the law which is to determine it *anywhere else* than in the fitness of its maxims to be universal laws of its own dictation, consequently if it goes out of itself and seeks this law in the character of any of its objects, there always results *heteronomy*. The will in that case does not give itself the law, rather the law is given by the object through its relation to the will. This relation, whether it rests on inclination or on representations of reason, only admits of hypothetical imperatives: I ought to do something *because I will something else*. On the contrary, the moral, and therefore categorical, imperative says: I ought to do such and such, even though I do not will anything else. For example, the former says: I ought not to lie if I will to retain my reputation; the latter says: I ought not to lie although it should not bring me the least discredit. The latter therefore must so far abstract from all objects that they shall have no *influence* on the will, in order that practical reason (the will) may not be restricted to administering an interest not belonging to it, but may simply show its own commanding authority as the supreme legislation. Thus, for example, I ought to endeavor to promote the happiness of others, not as if its realization involved any concern of mine (whether by immediate inclination or by any satisfaction indirectly gained through reason), but simply because a maxim which excludes it cannot be included as a universal law in one and the same volition.

Division of All Possible Principles of Morality from the Assumed Fundamental Concept of Heteronomy

Here as elsewhere human reason in its pure use, so long as it was not critically examined, has first tried all possible wrong ways before it succeeded in finding the one true way.

All principles which can be taken from this point of view are either *empirical* or *rational*. The **former**, drawn from the principle [442] of *happiness*, are built on physical or moral feelings; the **latter**, drawn from the principle of *perfection*, are built either on the rational conception of perfection as a possible effect, or on that of an independent perfection (the will of God) as the determining cause of our will.

Empirical principles are wholly incapable of serving as a foundation for moral laws. For the universality with which these should hold for all rational beings without distinction, the unconditional practical necessity which is thereby imposed on them, is lost when their foundation is taken from the *particular constitution of human nature* or the accidental circumstances in which it is placed. The principle of *private happiness*, however, is the most objectionable, not merely because it is false, and experience contradicts the supposition that prosperity is always proportioned to good conduct, nor yet merely because it contributes nothing to the establishment of morality—since it is quite a different thing to make someone happy and to make him good, or to make him prudent and sharp-sighted for his own interests, and to make him virtuous—but because the incentives it provides for morality are such as rather undermine it and destroy its sublimity, since they put the motives to virtue and to vice in the same class, and only teach us to make a better calculation, the specific difference between virtue and vice being entirely extinguished. On the other hand, as to moral feeling, this supposed special sense,[1] the appeal to it is indeed superficial when those who cannot *think* believe that *feeling* will help them out, even in what concerns universal law; and besides, feelings which naturally differ infinitely in degree cannot furnish a uniform standard of good and evil, nor has anyone a right to form judgments for others by his own feelings; nevertheless this moral feeling is nearer to morality and its dignity in this respect, that it pays virtue the honor of ascribing to her *immediately* the satisfaction and esteem we have for her, and does not, as it were, tell her to her face that we are not attached to her by her beauty but by our advantage.

[443]

Among the *rational* grounds of morality, the ontological conception of *perfection*, notwithstanding its defects, is better than the theological conception which derives morality from a Divine absolutely perfect will. The former is, no doubt, empty and indefinite, and consequently useless for finding in the boundless field of possible reality the greatest amount suitable for us; moreover, in attempting to distinguish specifically the reality of which we are now speaking from every other, it inevitably tends to turn in a circle and cannot avoid tacitly presupposing the morality which it is to explain; it is nevertheless preferable to the theological view, first, because we have no intuition of the Divine perfection, and can only deduce it from our own concepts, the most important of which is morality, and our explanation would thus be involved in a gross circle; and, in the next place, if we avoid this, the only notion of the Divine will remaining to us is a concept made up of the attributes of desire for glory and domination, combined with the awful representations of might and vengeance, and any system of morals erected on this foundation would be directly opposed to morality.

However, if I had to choose between the notion of the moral sense and that of perfection in general (two systems which at least do not weaken morality, although they are totally incapable of serving as its foundation), then I should decide for the latter, because it at least withdraws the decision of the question from the

---

1 I class the principle of moral feeling under that of happiness, because every empirical interest promises to contribute to our well-being by the agreeableness that a thing affords, whether it be immediately and without a view to profit, or whether profit be regarded. We must likewise, with [Francis] Hutcheson [(1694-1746), a leading British "moral sense" philosopher], class the principle of sympathy with the happiness of others under his assumed moral sense. [I.K.]

sensibility and brings it to the court of pure reason; and although even here it decides nothing, it at all events preserves the indeterminate idea (of a will good in itself) free from corruption, until it shall be more precisely defined.

For the rest I think I may be excused here from a detailed refutation of all these doctrines; that would only be superfluous labor, since it is so easy, and is probably so well seen even by those whose office requires them to decide for one of those theories (because their hearers would not tolerate suspension of judgment). But what interests us more here is to know that the prime foundation of morality laid down by all these principles is nothing but heteronomy of the will, and for this reason they must necessarily miss their aim.

In every case where an object of the will has to be supposed, in [444] order that the rule may be prescribed which is to determine the will, there the rule is simply heteronomy; the imperative is conditional, namely, *if* or *because* one wills this object, one should act so and so; hence it can never command morally, that is, categorically. Whether the object determines the will by means of inclination, as in the principle of private happiness, or by means of reason directed to objects of our possible volition generally, as in the principle of perfection, in either case the will never determines itself *immediately* by the representation of the action, but only by the influence which the foreseen effect of the action has on the will; *I ought to do something, on this account, because I will something else*; and here there must be yet another law assumed in me as its subject, by which I necessarily will this other thing, and this law again requires an imperative to restrict this maxim. For the influence which the representation of an object within the reach of our faculties can exercise on the will of the subject in consequence of its natural properties, depends on the nature of the subject, either the sensibility (inclination and taste) or the understanding and reason, the employment of which is by the peculiar constitution of their nature attended with satisfaction. It follows that the law would be, properly speaking, given by nature, and as such it must be known and proved by experience, and would consequently be contingent, and therefore incapable of being an apodictic practical rule, such as the moral rule must be. Not only so, but it is *inevitably only heteronomy*; the will does not give itself the law, but is given the law by a foreign incentive by means of a particular natural constitution of the subject adapted to receive it.

An absolutely good will, then, the principle of which must be a categorical imperative, will be indeterminate as regards all objects, and will contain merely the *form of volition as such*, and indeed as autonomy, that is to say, the capacity of the maxims of every good will to make themselves a universal law, is itself the only law which the will of every rational being imposes on itself, without needing to assume any incentive or interest as its ground.

How such a synthetic practical a priori *proposition is possible*, and why it is necessary, is a problem whose solution does not lie within the bounds of the metaphysics of morals; and we have not here affirmed its truth, much less professed to have a proof of it in our power. We simply showed by the development of the universally received concept of morality that an autonomy of the will is inevitably connected with it, or rather with its foundation. Whoever then holds morality to be anything real, and not a chimerical idea without any truth, must likewise admit the principle of it that is here assigned. This section, then, like the first, was merely analytic. Now to prove that morality is no phantom of the brain, which it cannot be if the categorical imperative and with it the autonomy of the will is true, and as an *a priori* principle absolutely necessary, this supposes the possibility of *a synthetic use of pure practical reason*, which, however, we cannot venture upon without first giving a critical examination of this faculty of reason. In the concluding section we shall give the principal outlines of this critical examination as far as is sufficient for our purpose.

[445]

Transition from the Metaphysics of Morals to the Critique of Pure Practical Reason

The Concept of Freedom Is the Key to the Explanation of the Autonomy of the Will

The *will* is a kind of causality belonging to living beings in so far as they are rational, and *freedom* would be this property of such causality that it can be efficient, independently of foreign causes *determining* it; just as *natural necessity* is the property that the causality of all nonrational beings has of being determined to activity by the influence of foreign causes.

The preceding definition of freedom is *negative*, and therefore unfruitful for insight regarding its essence; but it leads to a *positive* conception which is so much more full and fruitful. Since the concept of causality involves that of laws, according to which, by something that we call cause, something else, namely, the effect, must be produced; hence, although freedom is not a property of the will in accordance with natural laws, yet it is not for that reason lawless; on the contrary, it must be a causality acting according to immutable laws, but of a special kind; otherwise a free will would be an absurdity. Natural necessity is a heteronomy of efficient causes, for every effect is possible only according to this law—that something else determines the efficient cause to exert its causality. What else can freedom of the will be but autonomy, [447] that is, the property of the will to be a law to itself? But the proposition: The will is in every action a law to itself, only expresses the principle to act on no other maxim than that which can also have as an object itself as a universal law. Now this is precisely the formula of the categorical imperative and is the principle of morality, so that a free will and a will subject to moral laws are one and the same.[1]

On the hypothesis, then, of freedom of the will, morality together with its principle follows from it by mere analysis of the concept. However, the latter is a synthetic proposition, viz., an absolutely good will is that whose maxim can always include itself regarded as a universal law; for this property of its maxim can

---

1 See Henry Sidgwick, "The Kantian Conception of Free Will" in Appendix I for consideration of whether Kant equivocates on his notion of freedom.

never be discovered by analyzing the concept of an absolutely good will. Now such synthetic propositions are only possible in this way—that the two cognitions are connected together by their union with a third in which they are both to be found. The *positive* concept of freedom furnishes this third cognition, which cannot, as with physical causes, be the nature of the sensible world (in the concept of which we find conjoined the concept of something in relation as cause to *something else* as effect). We cannot now at once show what this third is to which freedom points us, and of which we have an idea *a priori*, nor can we make intelligible how the concept of freedom is shown to be legitimate from principles of pure practical reason, and with it the possibility of a categorical imperative; but some further preparation is required.

Freedom Must Be Presupposed as a Property of the Will of All Rational Beings

It is not enough to predicate freedom of our own will, from whatever reason, if we have not sufficient grounds for predicating the same of all rational beings. For as morality serves as a law for us only because we are *rational beings*, it must also hold for all rational beings; and as it must be deduced simply from the property of freedom, it must be shown that freedom also is a property of all rational beings. It is not enough, then, to prove it from certain [448] supposed experiences of human nature (which indeed is quite impossible, and it can only be shown *a priori*), but we must show that it belongs to the activity of all rational beings endowed with a will. Now I say every being that cannot act except *under the idea of freedom* is just for that reason from a practical point of view really free, that is to say, all laws which are inseparably connected with freedom have the same force for him as if his will had been shown to be free in itself by a proof theoretically conclusive.[1] Now I affirm that to every rational being which has a will we must attribute also the idea of freedom, under which alone he acts. For in such a being we conceive a reason that is practical, that is, has

---

1 I adopt this method of assuming freedom merely *as an idea* which rational beings suppose in their actions, in order to avoid the necessity of proving it in its theoretical aspect also. The former is sufficient for my purpose; for even though the speculative proof should not be made out, yet a being that cannot act except with the idea of freedom is bound by the same laws that would obligate a being who was actually free. Thus we can escape here from the onus which presses on the theory. [I.K.]

causality in reference to its objects. Now we cannot possibly conceive a reason consciously receiving direction from any other quarter with respect to its judgments, for then the subject would ascribe the determination of its judgment not to its own reason, but to an impulse. It must regard itself as the author of its principles independent of foreign influences. Consequently, as practical reason or as the will of a rational being it must regard itself as free, that is to say, the will of such a being cannot be a will of its own except under the idea of freedom. This idea must therefore in a practical point of view be ascribed to every rational being.

Of the Interest Attaching to the Ideas of Morality

We have finally reduced the definite conception of morality to the idea of freedom. This latter, however, we could not prove to be actually a property of ourselves or of human nature; only we saw [449] that it must be presupposed if we would conceive a being as rational and conscious of its causality in respect of its actions, that is, as endowed with a will; and so we find that on just the same grounds we must ascribe to every being endowed with reason and will this attribute of determining itself to action under the idea of its freedom.

Now it resulted also from the presupposition of this idea that we became aware of a law that the subjective principles of action, that is, its maxims, must also be so assumed that they can also hold as objective, that is, universal principles, and so serve as universal laws of our own giving. But why, then, should I subject myself to this principle and do so simply as a rational being, thus also subjecting to it all other beings endowed with reason? I will allow that no interest *impels* me to do this, for that would not give a categorical imperative, but I must *take* an interest in it and discern how it comes to pass; for this "ought" is properly a "will," which is valid for every rational being, provided only that reason determined his actions without any hindrance. But for beings that are in addition affected as we are by incentives of a different kind, namely, sensibility, and in whose case that is not always done which reason alone would do, for these that necessity is expressed only as an "ought," and the subjective necessity is different from the objective.

It seems, then, as if the moral law, that is, the principle of autonomy of the will, were properly speaking only presupposed in the idea of freedom, and as if we could not prove its reality and objective necessity independently. In that case we should still have gained something considerable by at least determining the true principle more exactly than had previously been done; but as regards its validity and the practical necessity of subjecting oneself to it, we should not have advanced a step. For we were asked why the universal validity of our maxim as a law must be the condition restricting our actions, and on what we ground the worth which we assign to this manner of acting—a worth so great that there cannot be any higher interest—and if we were asked further how it happens that it is by this alone a human being believes he [450] feels his own personal worth, in comparison with which that of an agreeable or disagreeable condition is to be regarded as nothing, to these questions we could give no satisfactory answer.

We find indeed sometimes that we can take an interest in a personal quality which does not involve interest in any external condition, provided this quality makes us capable of participating in the condition in case reason were to effect the allotment; that is to say, the mere being worthy of happiness can interest us of itself even without the motive of participating in this happiness. This judgment, however, is in fact only the effect of the importance of the moral law which we before presupposed (when by the idea of freedom we detach ourselves from every empirical interest); but that we ought to detach ourselves from these interests, that is, to consider ourselves as free in action and yet as subject to certain laws, so as to find a worth simply in our own person which can compensate us for the loss of everything that gives worth to our condition, this we are not yet able to discern in this way, nor do we see how it is possible so to act—in other words, *on what grounds the moral law obligates us.*

It must be freely admitted that there is a sort of circle here from which it seems impossible to escape. In the order of efficient causes we assume ourselves free, in order that in the order of ends we may conceive ourselves as subject to moral laws; and we afterwards conceive ourselves as subject to these laws because we have attributed to ourselves freedom of the will; for freedom and self-legislation of will are both autonomy, and therefore are reciprocal concepts, and for this very reason one must not be used to explain the other or give the reason of it, but at most only for logical purposes to reduce apparently different notions of the same object to one single concept (as we reduce different fractions of the same value to the lowest terms).

One resource remains to us, namely, to inquire whether we do not occupy different points of view when by means of freedom we think ourselves as causes efficient *a priori*, and when we represent ourselves in terms of our actions as effects which we see before our eyes.

It is a remark which needs no subtle reflection to make, but which we may assume that even the commonest understanding can make, although it be after its fashion by an obscure discern- [451] ment of judgment which it calls feeling, that all the representations that come to us involuntarily (as those of the senses) do not enable us to cognizc objects otherwise than as they affect us; so that we remain ignorant of what they may be in themselves, and consequently that as regards representations of this kind even with the closest attention and clearness that the understanding can apply to them, we can by them only attain to the cognition of *appearances*, never to that of *things in themselves*. As soon as this distinction has once been made (perhaps merely in consequence of the difference observed between the representations given us from without, and in which we are passive, and those that we produce simply from ourselves, and in which we show our own activity), then it follows of itself that we must admit and assume behind the appearance something else that is not an appearance, namely, the things in themselves; although we must admit that, as we can never be acquainted with them except as they affect us, wc can come no nearer to them, nor can we ever know what they are in themselves. This must furnish a distinction, however crude, between a *world of sense* and the *world of understanding*, of which the former may be different according to the difference of the sensible impressions in various observers, while the second which is its basis always remains the same. Even as to himself, a human being cannot pretend to cognize what he is in himself from the cognizance he has by internal sensation. For as he does not as it were create himself, and does not come by the concept of himself *a priori* but empirically, it naturally follows that he can obtain his information even about himself only by inner sense, and consequently only through the appearances of his nature and the way in which his consciousness is affected. At the same time, beyond these characteristics of his own subject, made up of mere appearances, he must necessarily suppose something else as their basis, namely, his *ego*, whatever its characteristics in itself may be. Thus in respect to mere perception and receptivity of sensations he must reckon himself as belonging to the *world of sense*; but in respect of whatever there may be of pure activity in him (that which reaches consciousness immediately and not through affecting the senses), he must reckon himself as belonging to the *intellectual world*, of which, however, he has no further cognizance.

The reflecting human being must come to such a conclusion with respect to all the things which can be presented to him; it is probably to be met with even in persons of the commonest understanding, who, as is well known, are very much inclined to suppose behind the objects of the senses something else invisible and acting of itself. They spoil it, however, by presently making the invisible again sensible, that is to say, wanting to make it an object of intuition, so that they do not become a whit the wiser.

Now a human being really finds in himself a faculty by which he distinguishes himself from everything else, even from himself as affected by objects, and that is *reason*. This, being pure spontaneity, is even elevated above the *understanding*. For although the latter is a spontaneity and does not, like sense, merely contain representations that arise when we are affected by things (and are therefore passive), yet it cannot produce from its activity any other concept than those which merely serve *to bring sensible representations under rules*, and thereby to unite them in one consciousness, and without this use of the sensibility it could think of nothing at all; whereas, on the contrary, reason shows so pure a spontaneity in the case of what I call "ideas" that it thereby far transcends everything that the sensibility can give it, and exhibits its most important function in distinguishing the world of sense from that of understanding, and thereby prescribing the limits of the understanding itself.

For this reason a rational being must regard himself *qua intelligence* (not from the side of his lower faculties) as belonging not to the world of sense, but to that of understanding; hence he has two points of view from which he can regard himself, and cognize laws of the exercise of his faculties, and consequently of all his actions; *first*, so far as he belongs to the world of sense, he finds himself subject to laws of nature (heteronomy); *second*, as belonging to the intelligible world, under laws which, being independent of nature, have their foundation not in experience but in reason alone.

As a rational being, and consequently belonging to the intelligible world, a human being can never think of the causality of his own will otherwise than of under the idea of freedom, for independence from the determining causes of the sensible world (an independence which reason must always ascribe to itself) is freedom. Now the idea of freedom is inseparably connected with the concept of *autonomy*, and this again with the universal principle of morality which is ideally the foundation of all actions of *rational* beings, just as the law of nature is of all appearances.

Now the suspicion is removed which we raised above, that there was a latent circle involved in our reasoning from freedom to autonomy, and from this to the moral law, viz., that we laid down the idea of freedom because of the moral law only that we might afterwards in turn infer the latter from freedom, and consequently we could assign no ground at all for this law, but could only present it as begging the question which well-disposed minds would gladly concede to us, but which we could never put forward as a provable position. For now we see that when we think of ourselves as free we transfer ourselves into the world of understanding as members of it, and cognize the autonomy of the will along with its consequence, morality; whereas, if we think of ourselves as under obligation, we regard ourselves as belonging to the world of sense, and at the same time to the world of understanding.

How Is a Categorical Imperative Possible?

Every rational being counts himself *qua* intelligence as belonging to the world of understanding, and it is only as an efficient cause belonging to that world that he calls his causality a *will*. On the other side, he is also conscious of himself as a part of the world of sense in which his actions, which are mere appearances [phenomena] of that causality, are displayed; we cannot, however, discern how they are possible from this causality which we do not cognize; but instead of that, these actions as belonging to the sensible world must be viewed as determined by other appearances, namely, desires and inclinations. If therefore I were only a member of the world of understanding, then all my actions would perfectly conform to the principle of autonomy of the pure will; if I were only a part of the world of sense, they would necessarily be assumed to conform wholly to the natural law of desires and inclinations, in other words, to the heteronomy of nature. (The former would rest on morality as the supreme principle, the latter on happiness.) Since, however, *the world of understanding contains the ground of the world of sense, and consequently of its laws also*, and accordingly gives the law to my will (which belongs wholly to the world of understanding) directly, and must be thought as doing so, it follows that, although on the one side I must regard myself as a being belonging to the world of sense, yet, on the other side, I must recognize myself, as an intelligence, as subject to the law of the world of understanding, that is, to reason, which contains this law in the idea of freedom, and therefore as subject

[454]

to the autonomy of the will; consequently I must regard the laws of the world of understanding as imperatives for me, and the actions which conform to them as duties.

And thus what makes categorical imperatives possible is this— that the idea of freedom makes me a member of an intelligible world, in consequence of which, if I were nothing else, all my actions *would* always conform to the autonomy of the will; but as I at the same time intuit myself as a member of the world of sense, they *ought* so to conform, and this *categorical* "ought" represents a synthetic *a priori* proposition, inasmuch as besides my will as affected by sensible desires there is added further the idea of the same will, but as belonging to the world of the understanding, pure and practical of itself, which contains the supreme condition according to reason of the former will; precisely as concepts of the understanding which of themselves signify nothing but regular form in general are added to the intuitions of sense, and in this way synthetic *a priori* propositions become possible, on which all cognitions of a nature rests.

The practical use of common human reason confirms this reasoning. There is no one, not even the most consummate villain, provided only that he is otherwise accustomed to the use of reason, who, when we set before him examples of honesty of purpose, of steadfastness in following good maxims, of sympathy and general benevolence (even combined with great sacrifices of advantages and comfort), does not wish that he might also possess these qualities. Only on account of his inclinations and impulses he cannot attain this in himself, but at the same time he wishes to be free from such inclinations which are burdensome to himself. He proves by this that he transfers himself in thought with a will free from the impulses of the sensibility into an order of things wholly different from that of his desires in the field of sensibility; since he cannot expect to obtain by that wish any gratification of his desires, nor any position which would satisfy any of his actual or imaginable inclinations (for this would destroy the preeminence of the very idea which wrests that wish from him), he can only expect a greater intrinsic worth of his own person. [455] This better person, however, he imagines himself to be when he transfers himself to the point of view of a member of the world of the understanding, to which he is involuntarily forced by the idea of freedom, that is, of independence from *determining* causes of the world of sense; and from this point of view he is conscious of a good will, which by his own confession constitutes the law for the evil will that he possesses as a member of the world of sense—

a law whose authority he recognizes while transgressing it. What he morally "ought" is then what he necessarily "would" as a member of the world of the understanding, and is conceived by him as an "ought" only inasmuch as he likewise considers himself as a member of the world of sense.

On the Extreme Boundary of All Practical Philosophy

All human beings attribute to themselves freedom of the will. Hence come all judgments upon actions as being such as *ought to have been done, although they have not been done.* However, this freedom is not a concept of experience, nor can it be so, since it still remains, even though experience shows the contrary of those requirements which, on supposition of freedom, are represented as its necessary consequences. On the other side, it is equally necessary that everything that takes place should be determined without exception according to laws of nature. This necessity of nature is likewise not an empirical concept, just for this reason, that it involves the notion of necessity and consequently of *a priori* cognition. But this concept of a system of nature is confirmed by experience; and it must even be inevitably presupposed if experience itself is to be possible, that is, a coherent cognition of the objects of sense resting on general laws. Therefore freedom is only an *idea* of reason, and its objective validity in itself is doubtful; while nature is a *concept of the understanding* which proves, and must necessarily prove, its reality in examples of experience.

There arises from this a dialectic of reason, since the freedom attributed to the will appears to contradict the necessity of nature, and, placed between these two ways, reason *for speculative purposes* finds the road of natural necessity much more beaten and more appropriate than that of freedom; yet for *practical purposes* the narrow footpath of freedom is the only one on which it is possible to make use of reason in our conduct; hence it is [456] just as impossible for the subtlest philosophy as for the commonest reason of human beings to argue away freedom. Philosophy must then assume that no real contradiction will be found between freedom and natural necessity of the same human actions, for it cannot give up the concept of nature any more than that of freedom.

Nevertheless, even though we should never be able to comprehend how freedom is possible, we must at least remove this apparent contradiction in a convincing manner. For if the thought of freedom contradicts either itself or nature, which is equally necessary, it must in competition with natural necessity be entirely given up.

It would, however, be impossible to escape this contradiction if the thinking subject, which seems to itself free, thought of itself *in the same sense* or in *the very same relation* when it calls itself free as when in respect of the same action it assumes itself to be subject to the law of nature. Hence it is an indispensable problem of speculative philosophy to show that its illusion respecting the contradiction rests on this, that we think of the human being in a different sense and relation when we call him free, and when we regard him as subject to the laws of nature as being part of nature. It must therefore show that not only *can* both these very well coexist, but that both must be thought *as necessarily united* in the same subject, since otherwise no reason could be given why we should burden reason with an idea which, though it may possibly *without contradiction* be reconciled with another that is sufficiently established, yet entangles us in a perplexity which sorely embarrasses reason in its theoretical use. This duty, however, belongs only to speculative philosophy, in order that it may clear the way for practical philosophy. The philosopher, then, has no option whether he will remove the apparent contradiction or leave it untouched; for in the latter case the theory respecting this would be *bonum vacans*[1] into the possession of which the fatalist would have a right to enter, and chase all morality out of its supposed domain as occupying it without title.

We cannot, however, as yet say that we are touching the bounds of practical philosophy. For the settlement of that controversy does not belong to it; it only demands from speculative reason that it should put an end to the discord in which it entangles itself in theoretical questions, so that practical reason may have rest and security from external attacks which might make the ground on which it desires to be built a matter of dispute.

[457]

The claims to freedom of will made even by common reason are founded on the consciousness and the admitted supposition that reason is independent of merely subjectively determined causes which together constitute what belongs to feeling only, and which consequently come under the general designation of sensibility. A human being considering himself in this way as an intelligence places himself thereby in a different order of things and in

---

1 A vacant good, i.e., something, such as a piece of property, belonging to no one.

a relation to determining grounds of a wholly different kind when on the one hand he thinks of himself as an intelligence endowed with a will, and consequently with causality, and when on the other he perceives himself as a phenomenon in the world of sense (as he really is also), and affirms that his causality is subject to external determination according to laws of nature. Now he soon becomes aware that both can hold good, and indeed, must hold good at the same time. For there is not the smallest contradiction in saying that a *thing in appearance* (belonging to the world of sense) is subject to certain laws on which the very same *as a thing* or being *in itself* is independent; and that he must represent and think of himself in this two-fold way, rests as to the first on the consciousness of himself as an object affected through the senses, and as to the second on the consciousness of himself as an intelligence, that is, as independent on sensible impressions in the use of his reason (in other words, as belonging to the world of understanding).

Hence it comes to pass that a human being claims the possession of a will which takes no account of anything that comes under the head of desires and inclinations, and on the contrary conceives actions as possible to him, indeed, even as necessary, which can only be done by disregarding all desires and sensible inclinations. The causality of such actions lies in him as an intelligence and in the laws of effects and actions [which depend] on the principles of an intelligible world, of which indeed he knows nothing more than that in it pure reason alone, independent of sensibility, gives the law; moreover, since it is only in that world, as an intelligence, that he is his proper self (being as a human being only the appearance of himself), those laws apply to him directly and categorically, so that the incitements of inclinations and appetites (in other words, the whole nature of the world of sense) cannot impair the laws of his volition as an intelligence. [458] Indeed, he does not even hold himself responsible for the former or ascribe them to his proper self, that is, his will; he only ascribes to his will any indulgence which he might yield them if he allowed them to influence his maxims to the prejudice of the rational laws of the will.

When practical reason *thinks* itself into a world of understanding, it does not thereby transcend its own limits, as it would if it tried to enter it by *intuition* or *feeling*. The former is only a negative thought in respect of the world of sense, which does not give any laws to reason in determining the will, and is positive only in this single point, that this freedom as a negative characteristic is at the same time conjoined with a (positive) capacity and even with a causality of reason, which we designate a will, namely, a capacity so to act that the principle of the actions shall conform to the essential character of a rational motive, that is, the condition that the maxim have universal validity as a law. But were it to borrow an *object of will*, that is, a motive, from the world of understanding, then it would overstep its bounds and pretend to be acquainted with something of which it knows nothing. The concept of a world of understanding is then only a *point of view* which reason finds itself compelled to take outside appearances *in order to think of itself as practical*, which would not be possible if the influences of sensibility had a determining power on the human being, but which is necessary unless he is to be denied the consciousness of himself as an intelligence, and consequently as a rational cause, active by means of reason, that is, operating freely. This thought certainly involves the idea of an order and a system of laws different from that of the mechanism of nature which belongs to the sensible world; and it makes necessary the concept of an intelligible world (that is to say, the whole system of rational beings as things in themselves). But it does not in the least authorize us to think of it further than as to its *formal* condition only, that is, the universality of the maxims of the will as laws, and consequently the autonomy of the latter, which alone is consistent with its freedom; whereas, on the contrary, all laws that refer to a definite object give heteronomy, which only belongs to laws of nature, and can apply to the sensible world.

[459] But reason would overstep all its bounds if it undertook to *explain how* pure reason can be practical, which would be exactly the same problem as to explain *how freedom is possible*.

For we can explain nothing but that which we can reduce to laws the object of which can be given in some possible experience. But freedom is a mere idea, the objective reality of which can in no way be shown according to laws of nature, and consequently not in any possible experience; and for this reason it can never be comprehended or understood because we cannot support it by any sort of example or analogy. It holds good only as a necessary hypothesis of reason in a being that believes itself conscious of a will, that is, of a faculty distinct from mere desire (namely, a faculty of determining itself to action as an intelligence, in other words, by laws of reason independently of natural instincts). Now where determination according to laws of nature ceases, there all *explanation* ceases also, and nothing remains but *defense*, that is, the removal of the objections of those who pretend to have seen deeper into the nature of things, and thereupon boldly declare freedom impossible. We can only point out to them that the supposed contradiction that they have discovered in it arises only from this, that in order to be able to apply the law of nature to human actions, they must necessarily consider a human being as an appearance; then when we demand of them that they should think of him *qua* intelligence as a thing in itself, they still persist in considering him in this respect also as an appearance. In this view it would no doubt be a contradiction to suppose the causality of the same subject (that is, his will) to be withdrawn from all the natural laws of the sensible world. But this contradiction disappears if they would only themselves reflect and admit, as reasonable, that behind the appearances there must also lie at their root (although hidden) the things in themselves, and that we cannot expect the laws of these to be the same as those that govern their appearances.

The subjective impossibility of explaining the freedom of the will is identical with the impossibility of discovering and explaining an interest[1] which a human being can take in the moral law. Nevertheless he does actually take an interest in it, the basis of which in us we call the moral feeling, which some have falsely assigned as the standard of our moral judgment, whereas it must rather be viewed as the *subjective* effect that the law exercises on the will, the objective principle of which is furnished by reason alone.

[460]

In order that a sensibly affected rational being should will that reason alone prescribes the "ought," it is no doubt requisite that reason should have a power *to infuse a feeling of pleasure* or satisfaction in the fulfillment of duty, that is to say, that it should have a causality by which it determines the sensibility according to its

---

1   Interest is that by which reason becomes practical, that is, a cause determining the will. Hence we say of rational beings only that they take an interest in a thing; nonrational beings only feel sensual appetites. Reason takes a direct interest in action, then, only when the universal validity of its maxims is alone sufficient to determine the will. Such an interest alone is pure. But if it can determine the will only by means of another object of desire or on the suggestion of a particular feeling of the subject, then reason takes only an indirect interest in the action; and as reason by itself without experience cannot discover either objects of the will or a special feeling actuating it, this latter interest would only be empirical, and not a pure rational interest. The logical interest of reason (namely, to extend its insight) is never direct, but presupposes purposes for which reason is used. [I.K.]

own principles. But it is quite impossible to discern, that is, to make it intelligible *a priori*, how a mere thought, which itself contains nothing sensible, can itself produce a sensation of pleasure or pain; for this is a particular kind of causality of which, as of every other causality, we can determine nothing whatever *a priori*; we must only consult experience about it. But as this cannot supply us with any relation of cause and effect except between two objects of experience, whereas in this case, although indeed the effect produced lies within experience, yet the cause is supposed to be pure reason acting through mere ideas which offer no object to experience, it follows that for us human beings it is quite impossible to explain how and why the *universality of the maxim as a law*, that is, morality, interests us. This only is certain, that it is not *because it interests us* that it has validity for us (for that would be heteronomy and dependence of practical reason on sensibility, namely, on a feeling as its principle, in which case it could never give moral laws), but that it interests us because it is valid for us as human beings, inasmuch as it had its source in our will as intelligences, in other words, in our proper self, *and what belongs to mere appearance is necessarily subordinated by reason to the nature of the thing in itself.*

[461]

The question, then, how a categorical imperative is possible, can be answered to the extent that we can assign the only hypothesis on which it is possible, namely, the idea of freedom; and we can also discern the necessity of this hypothesis, and this is sufficient for the *practical exercise* of reason, that is, for the conviction of the *validity of this imperative*, and hence of the moral law; but how this hypothesis itself is possible can never be discerned by any human reason. On the hypothesis, however, that the will of an intelligence is free, its *autonomy*, as the essential formal condition of its determination, is a necessary consequence. Moreover, this freedom of will is not merely quite *possible* as a hypothesis (not involving any contradiction to the principle of natural necessity in the connection of the phenomena of the sensible world) as speculative philosophy can show; but is without any further condition also *necessary* for a rational being who is conscious of a causality through reason, that is to say, a will (distinct from desires) as he makes that freedom in practice (that is, in idea) the condition of all his voluntary actions. But to explain how pure reason can be of itself practical without the aid of any incentive that could be derived from any other source, that is, how the mere principle of the *universal validity of all its maxims as laws* (which would certainly be the form of a pure practical reason) can of itself supply an incentive, without any matter (object) of the will in which one could antecedently take any interest; and how it can produce an interest which would be called purely *moral*; or in other words, *how pure reason can be practical*—to explain this is beyond the power of human reason, and all the labor and pains of seeking an explanation of it are lost.

It is just the same as if I sought to find out how freedom itself is possible as the causality of a will. For then I quit the ground of philosophical explanation, and I have no other to go upon. I [462] might indeed revel in the world of intelligences which still remains to me, but although I have an *idea* of it that is well founded, yet I have not the least *cognizance* of it, nor can I ever attain to such cognizance with all the efforts of my natural faculty of reason. It signifies only a something that remains when I have eliminated everything belonging to the world of sense from the actuating principles of my will, serving merely to keep in bounds the principle of motives taken from the field of sensibility; fixing its limits and showing that it does not contain everything within itself, but that there is more beyond it; but this something more I cognize no further. Of pure reason which frames this ideal, there remains after the abstraction of all matter, that is, cognition of objects, nothing but the form, namely, the practical law of the universality of the maxims, and in conformity with this the concept of reason in reference to a pure world of understanding as a possible efficient cause, that is, a cause determining the will. There must here be a total absence of incentives unless this idea of an intelligible world is itself the incentive, or that in which reason primarily takes an interest; but to make this intelligible is precisely the problem that we cannot solve.

Here now is the extreme limit of all moral inquiry, and it is of great importance to determine it even on this account in order that reason may not, on the one hand, to the detriment of morals, seek about in the world of sense for the supreme motive and an interest comprehensible but empirical; and on the other hand, that it may not impotently flap its wings without being able to move in the (for it) empty space of transcendent concepts which we call the intelligible world, and so lose itself amidst chimeras. For the rest, the idea of a pure world of understanding as a system of all intelligences, and to which we ourselves as rational beings belong (although we are also on the other side members of the sensible world), this remains always a useful and legitimate idea for the purposes of rational belief, although all cognition stops at its threshold, useful, namely, to produce in us a lively interest in the moral law by means of the noble ideal of a universal kingdom of *ends in themselves* (rational beings), to which we can belong as members then only when we carefully conduct ourselves according to the maxims of freedom as if they were laws of nature.

Concluding Remark

The speculative use of reason *with respect to nature* leads to the absolute necessity of some supreme cause of *the world*; the practical use of reason *with a view to freedom* leads also to absolute necessity, but only *of the laws of the actions* of a rational being as such. Now it is an essential *principle* of reason, however used, to push its knowledge to a consciousness of its necessity (without which it would not be rational cognition). It is, however, an equally essential *restriction* of the same reason that it can neither discern the *necessity* of what is or what happens, nor of what ought to happen, unless a condition is supposed on which it is or happens or ought to happen. In this way, however, by the constant inquiry for the condition, the satisfaction of reason is only further and further postponed. Hence it unceasingly seeks the unconditionally necessary, and finds itself forced to assume it, although without any means of making it comprehensible to itself, happy enough if only it can discover a conception which agrees with this assumption. It is therefore no fault in our deduction of the supreme principle of morality, but an objection that should be made to human reason in general, that it cannot enable us to conceive the absolute necessity of an unconditional practical law (such as the categorical imperative must be). It cannot be blamed for refusing to explain this necessity by a condition, that is to say, by means of some interest assumed as a basis, since the law would then cease to be a moral law, that is, a supreme law of freedom. And thus while we do not comprehend the practical unconditional necessity of the moral imperative, we yet comprehend its *incomprehensibility*, and this is all that can be fairly demanded of a philosophy which strives to carry its principles up to the very boundary of human reason.

Appendix A: Immanuel Kant, "An Answer to the Question: What is Enlightenment?" (1784)

[This essay originally appeared in the December 12, 1784 issue of *Berlinischen Monatsschrift*, in response to the question, "What is Enlightenment?" posed by an article in a previous issue. It is fitting that Kant addresses this question directly: the eighteenth century is considered the age of Enlightenment, and Kant is considered one of the foremost philosophers of the Enlightenment. The essay reveals Kant's views about the sort of freedom, and government, necessary for enlightenment. The translation is mine.]

Enlightenment is the human being's emergence from his self- [8:35] incurred immaturity. *Immaturity* is the inability to use one's understanding without the guidance of another. This immaturity is *self-incurred* if its cause lies not in lack of understanding, but in lack of resolution and lack of courage to use it without the guidance of another. *Sapere aude!*[1] Have courage to use your own understanding! is therefore the motto of enlightenment.

Laziness and cowardice are the reasons why such a large portion of humankind, after nature has long declared them free from foreign guidance (*naturaliter maiorennes*), nevertheless gladly remain immature for life; and why it becomes so easy for others to appoint themselves their guardians. It is so convenient to be immature! If I have a book that has understanding for me, a minister who has conscience for me, a doctor who evaluates my diet for me, and so on, I need not make any effort myself. I have no need to think, if only I can pay; others will soon enough take over the tiresome business for me. Those guardians who have kindly taken upon themselves the work of supervision will take care that by far the largest part of humankind (including the whole fair sex) should find that the step to maturity is, besides troublesome, also very dangerous. After they have first made their domesticated animals stupid and carefully prevented these docile creatures from daring to venture even one step out of the leading-strings to

---

1 Dare to be wise!

which they have bound them, they then show them the danger that threatens them if they try to walk alone. Now this danger is not actually so large, for they would certainly learn to walk well eventually after a few falls; but an example of this kind makes them timid and usually frightens them from further attempts.

[36]

Thus it is difficult for any separate *individual* to work his way out of the immaturity that has become almost second nature to him. He has even grown fond of it, and is really unable to use his own understanding for the time being, because he was never allowed to make the attempt. Rules and formulas, those mechanical instruments for rational use, or rather misuse of his natural endowments, are the ball and chain of his ever-lasting immaturity. And if anyone did cast them off, he would still be uncertain about leaping over even the narrowest of trenches, since he is not accustomed to free movement. Thus only a few, by their own cultivation of their minds, have succeeded in freeing themselves from immaturity, and in continuing boldly on their way.

There is more possibility of a *public* enlightening itself; indeed it is almost inevitable, if only the public is left in freedom, for there will always be a few who think for themselves, even among those appointed as guardians of the common mass, who, after they themselves have cast off the yoke of immaturity, will disseminate the spirit of rational valuing of one's own worth and of each human being's vocation to think for himself. But it should be noted that the public, which was previously put under this yoke by the guardians, if suitably stirred up by some of the latter who are incapable of enlightenment, may subsequently force the guardians themselves to remain under the yoke; so harmful is it to propagate prejudices, since they finally take revenge themselves on the very people who first cultivated them (or whose predecessors did). Thus a public can achieve enlightenment only slowly. Though a revolution may well put an end to personal despotism and to a voracious or power-seeking oppression, it will never produce a true reform in ways of thinking; rather, new prejudices will serve as well as old ones to control the great, unthinking mass.

For this enlightenment, however, nothing is needed but *freedom*; and indeed the most harmless of anything that could be called freedom: namely, freedom to make *public use* of one's own reason in all matters. But I hear on all sides the cry: *Do not argue!* The officer says: Do not argue, but drill! The tax official says: Do not argue, pay! The clergyman says: Do not argue, believe! (Only one ruler in the world says: *Argue* as must as you like and about

[37]

whatever you like, *but obey!*)[1] Everywhere there are restrictions on freedom. But which sort of restriction hinders enlightenment, and which does not hinder but instead promotes it? I answer: the *public use* of one's reason must always be free, and it alone can bring about enlightenment among human beings; the *private use* of reason may quite often be very narrowly restricted, however, without particularly hindering the progress of enlightenment. But by the public use of one's own reason I understand that use which someone makes of it *as a scholar before the entire reading public*. What I call the private use of reason is that which one may make of it in a particular *civil* post or office with which one is entrusted. Now in many affairs which affect the interests of the commonwealth, a certain mechanism is necessary, whereby some members of the commonwealth must behave merely passively, so that they may, by an artificial unanimity, be directed by the government for public ends, or at least deterred from destroying those ends. Here it is, of course, impermissible to argue; rather, one must obey. But insofar as this part of the machine also considers himself as a member of a whole commonwealth or even of a cosmopolitan society, and so in the role of a scholar who may through his writings address a public in the proper sense of the word, he may indeed argue without harming the affairs for which he is in part responsible as a passive member. Thus it would be very harmful if an officer receiving an order from his superiors wanted to debate openly, while on duty, about the appropriateness or usefulness of the order; instead, he must obey. But he cannot equitably be prevented from making remarks as a scholar on the errors of military service, and from offering these to his public for judgment. The citizen cannot refuse to pay the taxes imposed upon him; presumptuous criticisms of such taxes, when he is to pay them, may be punished as a scandal (which could lead to general insubordination). However, the same citizen does not contravene his duty as a citizen if, as a scholar, he publicly expresses his thoughts on the impropriety or even injustice of such fiscal measures. Similarly, a clergyman is obligated to [38] instruct his catechism students and his congregation in accordance with the doctrine of the church he serves; for he was employed by it on that condition. But as a scholar, he has complete freedom and even the vocation to communicate to the

---

1 Frederick the Great.

public all his carefully considered, well-intentioned thoughts on what is mistaken in that doctrine, and his suggestions for a better arrangement of the religious and ecclesiastical body. And there is in this nothing that can be laid as a burden on his conscience. For what he teaches in consequence of this office as an agent of the business of the church, he represents as something about which he does not have free power to teach according to his own discretion, but which he is appointed to expound in a prescribed manner and in the name of another. He will say: Our church teaches this or that; these are the arguments it uses. He then extracts all practical uses for his congregation from principles to which he would not himself subscribe with full conviction but which he can nevertheless undertake to expound, since it is still not wholly impossible that truth may lie hidden in them, and, in any case, there is at least nothing contradictory to inner religion present in them. For if he believed he had found the latter in them, he would not be able to hold his office in good conscience; he would have to give it up. The use therefore that an appointed teacher makes of his reason before his congregation is purely a *private use*; for this congregation is still only a domestic gathering, however large it is; and in view of this he, as a priest, is not free and cannot be free, because he carries out the commission of another. Conversely, as a scholar, who through his writings speaks to the real public, namely the world, a clergyman in the *public use* of his reason enjoys an unlimited freedom to use his own reason and to speak in his own person. For that the guardians of the people (in spiritual things) should themselves be immature is an absurdity that amounts to the perpetuation of absurdities.

But should not a society of clergymen, such as a church conference or a venerable classis (as it calls itself among the Dutch), be entitled to obligate itself by oath to a certain unalterable creed, in order to secure an unceasing guardianship over each of its members and through them over the people, and even to perpetuate this? I say that this is wholly impossible. Such a contract, made to deprive the human race of all further enlightenment forever, is absolutely null and void, even if it were ratified by the supreme power, by parliament and by the most solemn peace treaties. One age cannot obligate itself and vow to put the succeeding one into such a condition that it would be impossible for it to extend its cognitions (especially in such important matters) and to purify them of errors, and generally to progress in enlightenment. This would be *a crime against human nature*, whose orig-

[39]

inal destiny lies precisely in such progress; and succeeding generations are therefore perfectly justified in rejecting such decisions as unauthorized and made maliciously. The touchstone of whatever can be concluded as law for a people lies in the question: *whether a people could impose such a law on itself.* Now this might well be possible in expectation as it were of a better solution, for a determinate, short time, in order to introduce a certain order; during that time each citizen, particularly a clergyman, would be left free, in his capacity as a scholar, to make his comments publicly, i.e., though writings, about flaws in the current institution; meanwhile, the introduced order would last until public insight into the nature of these things had become so general and confirmed that through the unity of their voices (even if not all of them) it could bring a proposal to the throne, to take under its protection these congregations that have, perhaps, in accordance with their concepts of better insight, agreed to a changed religious establishment, without, however, hindering those that wanted to remain in the old one. But it is absolutely impermissible to agree, even for the lifetime of one human being, to a permanent religious constitution which is not to be questioned publicly by anyone and thereby, as it were, to nullify a period of time in the progress of humanity toward improvement, making it fruitless and even detrimental to subsequent generations. A human being can indeed, for his own person and even then only for a short time, postpone enlightenment in what he ought to know; but to renounce it whether for his own person or even more so for subsequent generations, is to violate the sacred right of humanity and trample it underfoot. What a people may never decide upon for itself, however, a monarch may even less decide upon for a people; for his legislative authority [40] rests precisely on this, that he unites the collective will of the people in his own. So long as he sees to it that any true or alleged improvement is compatible with civil order, he can otherwise leave it to his subjects to do what they find it necessary to do for the sake of their salvation; that is no concern of his, but it is indeed his concern to stop any one of them from forcibly hindering others from working to the best of their ability for the determination and promotion of their salvation. It even detracts from his majesty if he interferes in these matters by honoring with government supervision the writings in which his subjects try to clarify their insight, as well as if he does so from his own supreme insight, in which case he exposes himself to the reproach: *Caesar non est supra grammaticos*,[1] but much more so if he demeans his high authority so far as to support the ecclesiastical despotism of a few tyrants in his states against the rest of his subjects.

If it is now asked whether we now live in an *enlightened age*, the answer is: No, but we do live in an *age of enlightenment*. As things now stand, a good deal more is required for people on the whole to be in the position, or even able to be put into the position, of using their own understanding confidently and well in religious matters, without outside guidance. But we do have clear indications that the field is now being opened for them to work freely in this direction and that the hindrances to universal enlightenment or to humankind's emergence from its self-incurred immaturity are gradually becoming fewer. In this respect this age is the age of enlightenment or the century of Frederick.

A prince who does not find it beneath him to say that he considers it his *duty* not to prescribe anything to human beings in religious matters but to allow them complete freedom, who thus declines even the presumptuous name of *tolerance*, is himself enlightened and deserves to be praised by a grateful world and by posterity as the one who first liberated the human race from immaturity, at least from the side of government, and left each free to use his own reason in all matters of conscience. Under him, venerable clergymen, notwithstanding their official duties, may in their capacity as scholars freely and publicly submit their judgments and insights, deviating here and there from the estab-

[41] lished creed, to the world for examination; and even more may any other, who is restricted by no official duties. This spirit of freedom is also spreading abroad, even where it has to struggle with outer hindrances of a government that misunderstands itself. For it shines as an example for such a government that in freedom there is not the least cause for concern about public peace and the unity of the commonwealth. Human beings work their way out of barbarism gradually of their own accord if one only does not deliberately contrive to keep them in it.

I have placed the main point of enlightenment, of emergence of human beings from their self-incurred immaturity, chiefly in *religious matters*, because our rulers have no interest in playing guardian over their subjects with respect to the arts and sciences;

---

1 Caesar is not above the grammarians.

moreover, that immaturity being the most harmful, is also the most degrading of all. But the attitude of mind of a head of state who favors the first goes still further and sees that even with regard to his *legislation* there is no danger in allowing his subjects to make *public* use of their own reason and to publish to the world their thoughts about a better way of formulating it, even with a forthright critique of that already given; we have a shining example of this, in which no monarch has yet surpassed the one whom we honor.

But only one who, himself enlightened, is not afraid of shadows, but at the same time has a well-disciplined and numerous army ready to assure public peace, can say what a republic may not dare to say: *Argue as much as you will and about what you will; only obey!* Here is shown a strange and unexpected trend in human affairs, as also happens elsewhere if it is looked at in the large, where almost everything is paradoxical. A greater degree of civil freedom seems beneficial to a people's freedom of *mind* and yet also puts up insuperable barriers to it; a lesser degree of the former, on the other hand, provides room for the latter to expand to its full capacity. Thus when nature has uncovered, from under this hard shell, the seed for which she most tenderly cares, namely the propensity and vocation to *think* freely, the latter gradually works back upon the mentality of the people (which thereby gradually becomes capable of *freedom* in acting) and eventually [42] even upon the principles of *government*, which finds it advantageous to itself to treat the human being, *who is now more than a machine*, in accordance with his dignity.[1]

Königsberg in Prussia, September 30, 1784

---

1 In *Büschings Wöchentliche Nachrichten* of September 13th, I read today, September 30th, an announcement of this month's *Berlinischen Monatsschrift*, which mentions Mr. Mendelssohn's answer to the same question. This journal has not yet come to me; otherwise I would have held back the present essay, which may now stand only in order to see to what extent chance may bring about agreement in thoughts. [I.K.]

Appendix B: From Immanuel Kant, Critique of Practical Reason (1788)

[The *Critique of Practical Reason* is in large part Kant's attempt to correct what he saw as misinterpretations of his views in the third section of the *Groundwork* (which he had described as "a critique of practical reason"), and to develop and defend these views through some new arguments. The *Critique of Practical Reason* clarifies the relation between reason's practical and theoretical employments, defends the existence of freedom, immortality, and God as "practical postulates," and provides what Kant calls a "credential" for the moral law. The following selections focus on Kant's conception of the highest good, the relation of virtue to happiness within the highest good, and practical arguments for belief in immortality and God based on reason's need to believe in the possible realization of the highest good.

The translation is by T.K. Abbott, originally published in 1909, based on the Rosenkranz and Schubert edition of Kant's complete works. I have made only minor revisions and added Prussian Academy pagination.]

Book II, Chapter II—Of the Dialectic of Pure Reason in Defining the Conception of the Highest Good [5:110]

The conception of the *highest* itself contains an ambiguity which might occasion needless disputes if we did not attend to it. The highest may mean either the supreme (*supremum*) or the perfect (*consummatum*). The former is that condition which is itself unconditioned, i.e., is not subordinate to any other (*originarium*); the second is that whole which is not a part of a greater whole of the same kind (*perfectissimum*). It has been shown in the Analytic that *virtue* (as worthiness to be happy) is the *supreme condition* of all that can appear to us desirable, and consequently of all our pursuit of happiness, and is therefore the *supreme* good. But it does not follow that it is the whole and perfect good as the object of the desires of rational finite beings; for this requires *happiness* also, and that not merely in the partial eyes of the person who makes himself an end, but even in the judgment of an impartial reason, which regards persons in general as ends in themselves.

For to need happiness, to deserve it, and yet at the same time not to participate in it, cannot be consistent with the perfect volition of a rational being possessed at the same time of all power, if, for the sake of experiment, we conceive such a being. Now inasmuch as virtue and happiness together constitute the possession of the highest good in a person, and the distribution of happiness in exact proportion to morality (which is the worth of the person, and his worthiness to be happy) constitutes the *highest good* of a [111] possible world; hence this highest good expresses the whole, the perfect good, in which, however, virtue as the condition is always the supreme good, since it has no condition above it; whereas happiness, while it is pleasant to the possessor of it, is not itself absolutely and in all respects good, but always presupposes morally right behavior as its condition.

When two elements are *necessarily* united in one concept, they must be connected as ground and consequent, and this either so that their *unity* is considered as *analytical* (logical connection), or as synthetical (real *connection*)—the former following the law of identity, the latter that of causality. The connection of virtue and happiness may therefore be understood in two ways: either the endeavor to be virtuous and the rational pursuit of happiness are not two distinct actions, but absolutely identical, in which case no maxim need be made the principle of the former, other than what serves for the latter; or the connection consists in this, that virtue produces happiness as something distinct from the consciousness of virtue, as a cause produces an effect.

The ancient Greek schools were, properly speaking, only two, and in determining the conception of the highest good these followed in fact one and the same method, inasmuch as they did not allow virtue and happiness to be regarded as two distinct elements of the highest good, and consequently sought the unity of the principle by the rule of identity; but they differed as to which of the two was to be taken as the fundamental notion. The Epicurean[1] said: To be conscious that one's maxims lead to happiness is virtue; the Stoic[2] said: To be conscious of one's virtue is happiness. With the former, *prudence* was equivalent to morality; with the latter, who chose a higher designation for virtue, *morality* alone was true wisdom.

---

1 Epicureanism was a school of Greek philosophy founded in 306 BCE by Epicurus (341-270 BCE).
2 Stocism was a school of Greek philosophy founded circa 300 BCE by Zeno (335-263 BCE).

While we must admire the men who in such early times tried all imaginable ways of extending the domain of philosophy, we must at the same time lament that their acuteness was unfortunately misapplied in trying to trace out identity between two extremely heterogeneous notions, those of happiness and virtue.... [112]

While both schools sought to trace out the identity of the practical principles of virtue and happiness, they were not agreed as to the way in which they tried to force this identity, but were separated infinitely from one another, the one placing its principle on the side of feeling, the other on that of reason; the one in the consciousness of sensible wants, the other on the independence of practical reason from all sensible grounds of determination. According to the Epicurean the notion of virtue was already involved in the maxim: To promote one's own happiness; according to the Stoics, on the other hand, the feeling of happiness was already contained in the consciousness of virtue. Now whatever is contained in another notion is identical with part of the containing notion, but not with the whole, and moreover two wholes may be specifically distinct, although they consist of the same parts, namely, if the parts are united into a whole in totally different ways. The Stoic maintained that virtue was the *whole highest good*, and happiness only the consciousness of possessing it, as making part of the state of the subject. The Epicurean maintained that happiness was the *whole highest good*, and virtue only the form of the maxim for its pursuit, viz., the rational use of the means to attaining it.

Now it is clear from the Analytic that the maxims of virtue and those of private happiness are quite heterogeneous as to their supreme practical principle; and although they belong to one highest good which together they make possible, yet they are so far from coinciding that they restrict and check one another very much in the same subject. Thus the question, *How is the highest good practically possible?* still remains an unsolved problem, notwithstanding all the *attempts at coalition* that have hitherto been made. The Analytic has, however, shown what it is that makes the problem difficult to solve; namely, that happiness and morality are two specifically *distinct elements* of the highest good, and therefore their combination cannot be *analytically* cognized (as if someone who seeks his own happiness should find by mere   [113]
analysis of his conception that in so acting he is virtuous, or as if someone who follows virtue should in the consciousness of such conduct find that he is already happy *ipso facto*), but must be a

synthesis of concepts. Now since this combination is recognized as *a priori*, and therefore as practically necessary, and consequently not as derived from experience, so that the possibility of the highest good does not rest on any empirical principle, it follows that the *deduction* of this concept must be *transcendental*. It is *a priori* (morally) necessary *to produce the highest good by freedom of the will*; therefore the condition of its possibility must rest solely on *a priori* principles of cognition.

I. The Antinomy of Practical Reason[1]

In the highest good which is practical for us, i.e., to be realized by our will, virtue and happiness are thought as necessarily combined, so that the one cannot be assumed by practical reason without the other also being attached to it. Now this combination (like every other) is either *analytical* or *synthetical*. It has been shown that it cannot be analytical; it must then be synthetical, and, more particularly, must be conceived as the connection of cause and effect, since it concerns a practical good, i.e., one that is possible by means of action; consequently either the desire for happiness must be the motive to maxims of virtue, or the maxim of virtue must be the efficient cause of happiness. The first is *absolutely* impossible because (as was proved in the Analytic) maxims which place the determining principle of the will in the desire for personal happiness are not moral at all, and no virtue can be found in them. But the second is *also impossible*, because the practical connection of causes and effects in the world, as the result of the determination of the will, does not depend upon the moral disposition of the will, but on the knowledge of the laws of nature and the physical power to use them for one's purposes; consequently we cannot expect in the world by the most punctilious observance of the moral laws any necessary connection of

---

1 Kant's antinomies present arguments for two contradictory propositions. They are designed to illustrate the contradictions reason falls into when it fails to recognize its own bounds. In this case, the opposing propositions are "the desire for happiness must be the motive to maxims of virtue" and "the maxim of virtue must be the efficient cause of happiness." Kant argues that neither proposition can be true—unless we distinguish between appearances and things in themselves. In Kant's solution to this antinomy, he refers to the third antinomy in the *Critique of Pure Reason* (A445-51/B473-79), which concerns freedom and natural causality.

happiness with virtue adequate to the highest good. Now as the [114] promotion of this highest good, the conception of which contains this connection, is *a priori* a necessary object of our will, and inseparably attached to the moral law, the impossibility of the former must prove the falsity of the latter. If then the supreme good is not possible by practical rules, then the moral law also which commands us to promote it is directed to vain imaginary ends, and must consequently be false.

II. Critical Solution of the Antinomy of Practical Reason

The antimony of pure speculative reason exhibits a similar conflict between freedom and physical necessity in the causality of events in the world. It was solved by showing that there is no real contradiction when the events and even the world in which they occur are regarded (as they ought to be) merely as appearances; since one and the same acting being, as an *appearance* (even to his own inner sense), has a causality in the world of sense that always conforms to the mechanism of nature, but with respect to the same events, so far as the acting person regards himself at the same time as a *noumenon* (as pure intelligence in an existence not dependent on the condition of time), he can contain a principle by which that causality acting according to laws of nature is determined, but which is itself free from all laws of nature.

It is just the same with the foregoing antinomy of pure practical reason. The first of the two propositions—That the endeavor after happiness produces a virtuous mind, is *absolutely false*; but the second, That a virtuous mind necessarily produces happiness is *not absolutely* false, but only in so far as virtue is considered as a form of causality in the sensible world, and consequently only if I suppose existence in it to be the only sort of existence of a rational being; it is then only *conditionally false*. But as I am not only justified in thinking that I exist also as a noumenon in a world of the understanding, but even have in the moral law a [115] purely intellectual determining principle of my causality (in the sensible world) if not immediate yet mediate (viz., through an intelligent author of nature), and moreover necessary; while in a system of nature which is merely an object of the senses this combination could never occur except contingently, and therefore could not suffice for the highest good.

Thus, notwithstanding this seeming conflict of practical reason with itself, the highest good, which is the necessary supreme end of a will morally determined, is a true object thereof; for it is practically possible, and the maxims of the will which as regards their matter refer to it have objective reality, which at first was threatened by the antinomy that appeared in the connection of morality with happiness by a general law; but this was merely from a misconception, because the relation between appearances was taken for a relation of the things in themselves to these appearances.

....

[119] From this solution of the antinomy of pure practical reason it follows that in practical principles we may at least conceive as possible a natural and necessary connection between the consciousness of morality and the expectation of a proportionate happiness as its result, though it does not follow that we can know or perceive this connection; that, on the other hand, principles of the pursuit of happiness cannot possibly produce morality; that, therefore, morality is the supreme good (as the first condition of the highest good), while happiness constitutes its second element, but only in such a way that it is the morally conditioned but necessary consequence of the former. Only with this subordination is the highest good the whole object of pure practical reason, which must necessarily conceive it as possible, since it commands us to contribute to the utmost of our power to its realization. But since the possibility of such connection of the conditioned with its condition belongs wholly to the supersensual relation of things, and cannot be given according to the laws of the world of sense, although the practical consequences of the idea belong to the world of sense, namely, the actions that aim at realizing the highest good; we will therefore endeavor to set forth the grounds of that possibility, first, in respect of what is immediately in our power, and then, secondly, in that which is not in our power, but which reason presents to us as the supplement of our impotence, for the realization of the highest good (which by practical principles is necessary).

III. Of the Primacy of Pure Practical Reason in Its Union with Speculative Reason

By primacy between two or more things connected by reason, I understand the prerogative belonging to one, of being the first determining principle in the connection with all the rest. In a narrower practical sense it means the prerogative of the interest of one in so far as the interest of the other is subordinated to it, while it is not postponed to any other. To every faculty of the mind we can attribute an *interest*, that is a principle that contains the condition on which alone the former is called into exercise.

Reason, as the faculty of principles, determines the interest of all [120] the powers of the mind, and is determined by its own. The interest of its speculative employment consists in the *cognition* of the object pushed to the highest *a priori* principles: that of its practical employment, in the determination of the *will* in respect of the final and complete end. As to what is necessary for the possibility of any employment of reason at all, namely, that its principles and affirmations should not contradict one another, this constitutes no part of its interest, but is the condition of having reason at all; it is only its development, not mere consistency with itself, that is reckoned as its interest.

If practical reason could not assume or think as given anything further than what speculative reason of itself could offer it from its own insight, the latter would have primacy. But supposing that it had of itself original *a priori* principles with which certain theoretical positions were inseparably connected, while these were withdrawn from any possible insight of speculative reason (which, however, they must not contradict); then the question is, which interest is the superior (not which must give way, for they are not necessarily conflicting), whether speculative reason, which knows nothing of all that practical reason offers for its acceptance should take up these propositions, and (although they transcend it) try to unite them with its own concepts as a foreign possession handed over to it, or whether it is justified in obstinately following its own separate interest, and according to the canonic of Epicurus rejecting as vain subtlety everything that cannot accredit its objective reality by manifest examples to be shown in experience, even though it should be never so much interwoven with the interest of the practical (pure) use of reason, and in itself not contradictory to the theoretical, merely because it infringes on the interest of the speculative reason to this extent, that it removes the bounds which this latter had set to itself, and gives it up to every nonsense or delusion of imagination?

In fact, so far as practical reason is taken as dependent on pathological conditions, that is, as merely regulating the inclinations under the sensible principle of happiness, we could not require speculative reason to take its principles from such a source. Mohammed's paradise, or the absorption into the Deity of the theosophists[1] and mystics, would press their monstrosities [121]

---

1 Theosophists believe they can apprehend God's nature directly, independently of revelation.

on reason according to the taste of each, and one might as well have no reason as surrender it in such fashion to all sorts of dreams. But if pure reason of itself can be practical and is actually so, as the consciousness of the moral law proves, then it is still only one and the same reason which, whether in a theoretical or a practical point view, judges according to *a priori* principles; and then it is clear that although it is in the first point of view incompetent to establish certain propositions positively, which, however, do not contradict it, then *as soon as these propositions are inseparably attached to the practical interest* of pure reason, it must accept them, though it be as something offered to it from a foreign source, something that has not grown on its own ground, but yet is sufficiently authenticated; and it must try to compare and connect them with everything that it has in is power as speculative reason. It must remember, however, that these are not additions to its insight, but yet are extensions of its employment in another, namely, a practical aspect; and this is not in the least opposed to its interest, which consists in the restriction of wild speculation.

Thus, when pure speculative reason and pure practical reason are combined in one cognition, the latter has the primacy, provided, namely, that this combination is not *contingent* and arbitrary, but founded *a priori* on reason itself and therefore *necessary*. For without this subordination there would arise a conflict of reason with itself; since if they were merely juxtaposed (coordinate), the former would close its boundaries strictly and admit nothing from the latter into its domain, while the latter would extend its bounds over everything, and when its needs required would seek to embrace the former within them. Nor could we reverse the order, and require pure practical reason to be subordinate to speculative reason, since all interest is ultimately practical, and even that of speculative reason is conditional, and it is only in the practical employment of reason that it is complete.

[122]   IV. The Immortality of the Soul as a Postulate of
Pure Practical Reason

The realization of the highest good in the world is the necessary object of a will determinable by the moral law. But in this will the *perfect accordance* of the mind with the moral law is the supreme condition of the highest good. This then must be possible, as well as its object, since it is contained in the command to promote the latter. Now, the perfect accordance of the will with the moral law is *holiness*, a perfection of which no rational being of the sensible world is capable at any moment of his existence. Since, nevertheless, it is required as practically necessary, it can only be found in an *endless progress* towards that perfect accordance, and on the principles of pure practical reason it is necessary to assume such a practical progress as the real object of our will.

Now, this endless progress is only possible on the supposition of an *endless* duration of the *existence* and personality of the same rational being (which is called immortality of the soul). The highest good, then, practically is only possible on the supposition of the immortality of the soul; consequently this immortality, being inseparably connected with the moral law, is a postulate of pure practical reason (by which I mean a *theoretical* proposition, not demonstrable as such, but which is an inseparable result of an unconditional *a priori practical* law).

This principle of the moral destination of our nature, namely that it is only in an endless progress that we can attain perfect accordance with the moral law, is of the greatest use, not merely for the present purpose of supplementing the impotence of speculative reason, but also with respect to religion. In default of it, either the moral law is quite degraded from its *holiness*, being made out to be lenient (indulgent), and conformable to our convenience, or else strains our notion of our vocation and our expectation to an unattainable goal, hoping to acquire complete holiness of will, and so lose ourselves in fantastical *theo-sophic* dreams, which wholly contradict self-knowledge. In both [123] cases the unceasing *effort* to obey punctually and thoroughly a strict and inflexible command of reason, which yet is not ideal but real, is only hindered. For a rational but finite being, the only thing possible is an endless progress from the lower to the higher degrees of moral perfection. *The Infinite Being*, to whom the condition of time is nothing, sees in this to us endless succession a whole of accordance with the moral law; and the holiness which His command inexorably requires, in order to be true to His justice in the share which He assigns to each in the highest good, is to be found in a single intellectual intuition of the whole existence of rational beings. All that can be expected of the creature in respect of the hope of this participation would be the consciousness of his tried character, by which, from the progress he has hitherto made from the worse to the morally better, and the immutability of purpose which has thus become known to him, he may hope for a further unbroken continuance of the same, however long his existence may last, even beyond

this life,[1] and thus he may hope, not indeed here, nor in any imaginable point of his future existence, but only in the endlessness of his duration (which God alone can survey) to be per-
[124] fectly adequate to his will (without indulgence or excuse, which do not harmonize with justice).

V. The Existence of God as a Postulate of Pure Practical Reason

In the foregoing analysis the moral law led to a practical problem which is prescribed by pure reason alone, without the aid of any sensible motives, namely, that of the necessary completeness of the first and principal element of the highest good, viz., **morality**; and as this can be perfectly solved only in eternity, to the postulate of *immortality*. The same law must also lead us to affirm the possibility of the second element of the highest good, viz., **happiness** proportioned to morality, and this on grounds as disinterested as before, and solely from impartial reason; that is, it must lead to the supposition of the existence of a cause adequate to this effect; in other words, it must postulate the *existence of God*, as the necessary condition of the possibility of the highest good (an object of the will which is necessarily connected with the moral legislation of pure reason). We proceed to exhibit this connection in a convincing manner.

Happiness is the condition of a rational being in the world with whom *everything goes according to his wish and will*; it rests, therefore, on the harmony of physical nature with his whole end, and likewise with the essential determining principle of his will. Now the moral law as a law of freedom commands by determining principles, which ought to be quite independent of nature and of its harmony with our faculty of desire (as incentives). But the acting rational being in the world is not the cause of the world and of nature itself. There is not the least ground, therefore, in the moral law for a necessary connection between morality and proportionate happiness in a being that belongs to the world as part of it, and therefore depends on it, and which for that reason cannot by his will be a cause of this nature, nor by his own power

1 It seems, nevertheless, impossible for a creature to have the conviction of his unwavering firmness of mind in the progress towards goodness. On this account the Christian religion makes it come only from the same Spirit that works sanctification, that is, this firm purpose, and with it the conscientiousness of steadfastness in the moral progress.... [I.K.]

make it thoroughly harmonize, as far as his happiness is concerned, with his practical principles. Nevertheless, in the practical problem of pure reason, i.e., the necessary pursuit of the high- [125] est good, such a connection is postulated as necessary: we *ought* to endeavor to promote the highest good, which, therefore, must be possible. Accordingly, the existence of a cause of all nature, distinct from nature itself, and containing the principle of this connection, namely, of the exact harmony of happiness with morality, is also *postulated*. Now, this supreme cause must contain the principle of the harmony of nature, not merely with a law of the will of rational beings, but with the conception of this *law*, insofar as they make it the *supreme determining principle of the will*, and consequently not merely with the form of morals, but with their morality as their motive, that is, with their moral character. Therefore, the highest good is possible in the world only on the supposition of a supreme cause of nature, having a causality corresponding to moral character. Now a being that is capable of acting on the conception of laws is *an intelligence* (a rational being), and the causality of such a being according to this conception of laws is his *will*; therefore the supreme cause of nature, which must be presupposed as a condition of the highest good, is a being which is the cause of nature by *intelligence* and *will*, consequently its author, that is, **God**. It follows that the postulate of the possibility of the *highest derived good* (the best world) is likewise the postulate of the *highest original good*, that is to say, of the existence of God. Now it was seen to be a duty for us to promote the highest good; consequently it is not merely allowable, but is a necessity connected with duty as a requisite, that we should presuppose the possibility of this highest good; and as this is possible only on condition of the existence of God, it inseparably connects the supposition of this with duty; that is, it is morally necessary to assume the existence of God.

It must be remarked here that this moral necessity *is subjective*, that is, it is a need, and not *objective*, that is, itself a duty, for there cannot be a duty to suppose the existence of anything (since this concerns only the theoretical employment of reason). Moreover, it is not meant by this that it is necessary to suppose the existence of God *as a basis of all obligation in general* (for this rests, as has been sufficiently proved, simply on the autonomy of reason [126] itself). What belongs to duty here is only the endeavor to realize and promote the highest good in the world, the possibility of which can therefore be postulated; and as our reason finds it not conceivable except on the supposition of a supreme intelligence, the admission of this existence is therefore connected with the consciousness of our duty, although the admission itself belongs to the domain of speculative reason. Considered in respect of this alone, as a principle of explanation, it may be called a *hypothesis*, but in reference to the intelligibility of an object given us by the moral law (the highest good), and consequently of a requirement for practical purposes, it may be called *faith*, that is to say a pure *rational faith*, since pure reason (both in this theoretical and its practical use) is the sole source from which it springs.

From this *deduction* it is now intelligible why the *Greek* schools could never attain the solution of their problem of the practical possibility of the highest good, because they made the rule of the use which the human will makes of his freedom the sole and sufficient ground of this possibility, thinking that they had no need for that purpose of the existence of God. No doubt they were so far right that they established the principle of morals of itself independently of this postulate, from the relation of reason only to the will, and consequently made it the *supreme* practical condition of the highest good; but it was not therefore the *whole* condition of its possibility. The Epicureans had indeed assumed as the supreme principle of morality a wholly false one, namely that of happiness, and had substituted for a law a maxim of arbitrary choice of each one according to his inclination; they proceeded, however, *consistently* enough in this, that they degraded their highest good likewise just in proportion to the meanness of their fundamental principle, and looked for no greater happiness than can be attained by human prudence (including temperance and moderation of the inclinations), and this, as we know, would be scanty enough and would be very different according to circumstances; not to mention the exceptions that their maxims must perpetually admit and which make them incapable of being laws. The Stoics, on the contrary, had chosen their supreme practical principle quite rightly, making virtue the condition of the highest good; but when they represented the degree of virtue required by its pure [127] law as fully attainable in this life, they not only strained the moral powers of the *human being* whom they called a *sage* beyond all the limits of his nature, and assumed a thing that contradicts all our knowledge of human beings, but also and principally they would not allow the second *element* of the highest good, namely happiness, to be properly a special object of human desire, but made their *sage*, like a divinity in his consciousness of the excellence of his person, wholly independent of nature (as regards his own contentment); they exposed him indeed to the evils of life, but made him not subject to them (at the same time representing him also as free from moral evil). They thus, in fact, left out the second element of the highest good, namely, personal happiness, placing it solely in action and satisfaction with one's own personal worth, thus including it in the consciousness of being morally minded, in which they might have been sufficiently refuted by the voice of their own nature.

Appendix C: From Immanuel Kant, "On the Common Saying: 'This May Be True in Theory, but It Does Not Apply in Practice'" (1793)

["On the Common Saying: 'This May Be True in Theory, but It Does Not Apply in Practice'" was first published in the September 1793 issue of *Berlinische Monatsschrift*. This selection contains most of Part 1, in which Kant defends his moral principle and his view of moral motivation against the criticisms of another Enlightenment philosopher, Christian Garve. Part 2 responds to Hobbes's views on the social contract as expressed in *De Cive* (1642) and *Leviathan* (1651). Part 3 responds to Mendelssohn's views on human progress as expressed in *Jerusalem, oder über religiöse Macht und Judentum* (1783).

From *Kant: Practical Philosophy*, edited and translated by Mary J. Gregor, Cambridge UP, 1996.[1] Reprinted with the permission of Cambridge UP.]

On the Relation of Theory [to] Practice in Morals Generally   [8:278]
(In reply to some objections by Professor Garve[2])

Before I come to the real point of controversy over what, in the use of one and the same concept, may be valid in theory only or in practice, I must compare my theory, as I have elsewhere represented it, with the representation of it that Garve gives, in order to see in advance whether we even understand each other.

A. I explained morals provisionally as the introduction to a science that teaches, not how we are to become happy, but how we

---

1 Gregor translates the title of the essay as "On the Common Saying: That May Be Correct in Theory, but It Is of No Use in Practice."

2 *Versuche über verschiedne Gegenstände aus der Moral und Literatur von Ch. Garve ...* [*Essays on Various Topics from Morality and Literature*, by Christian Garve, Part 1, pp. 111-16. (M.J.G.)]I call this worthy man's contesting of my propositions *objections* to matters in which (as I hope) he wishes to reach agreement with me, not attacks, which, as disparaging assertions, should provoke a defense; this is not the place to defend them nor am I inclined to do so here. [I.K.]

are to become worthy of happiness.[1] In doing so I did not fail to remark that the human being is not thereby required to *renounce* his natural end, happiness, when it is a matter of complying with his duty; for that he cannot do, just as no finite rational being whatever can; instead, he must *abstract* altogether from this consideration when the command of duty arises; he must on no [279] account make it the *condition* of his compliance with the law prescribed to him by reason; indeed he must, as far as is possible for him, strive to become aware that no *incentive* derived from that gets mixed, unnoticed, into the determination of duty, and this is effected by his representing duty as connected with the sacrifices its observance (virtue) costs us rather than with the advantages it yields us, so as to represent the command of duty in all its authority, as requiring unconditional obedience, sufficient in itself and in need of no other influences.

a. Now, the way Garve expresses this proposition of mine is that "I had maintained that observance of the moral law, without any regard for happiness at all, is the *sole final end* for the human being, that is must be considered the creator's sole end." (According to my theory, neither human morality by itself nor human happiness by itself is the creator's sole end, but rather the highest good possible in the world, which consists of the union and harmony of the two.)

B. I remarked further that this concept of duty does not have to be grounded on any particular end but rather *introduces* another end for the human being's will, namely to work to the best of one's ability toward the *highest good* possible in the world (universal human happiness combined with and in conformity with the purest morality throughout the world), which, since it is within our control from one quarter but not from both taken together, exacts from reason belief, *for practical purposes*, in a moral ruler of the world and a future life. It is not as if the universal concept of duty first gets "support and stability" only on the presupposition of both, that is, gets a sure basis and the requisite strength of an

---

1 Worthiness to be happy is that quality of a person, based upon the subject's own will, such that a reason giving universal laws (for nature as well as for free will) would harmonize with all the ends of this person. It is therefore quite different from skill in acquiring some happiness. For he is not even worthy of this skill and of the talents nature has lent him for it if he has a will which does not harmonize with that will which alone is adapted to a universal legislation of reason and which cannot be included in it (i.e., which conflicts with morality). [I.K.]

incentive, but rather that only in that ideal of pure reason does it also get an *object*.[1] For, in itself duty is nothing other than the *limitations* of the will to the condition of a giving of universal law possible through a maxim adopted, whatever the object of the will or the end may be (thus happiness as well), from which, as well as from every end one may have, we here abstract altogether. In the question of the *principle* of morals the doctrine of the *highest good*, as the final end of a will determined by this doctrine and conformed with its laws, can be completely passed over and set aside (as episodic); and it will also become apparent in what follows, when it comes to the real point of controversy, that this is not taken into consideration at all but only morals in general.

---

1 The need to assume, as the final end of all things, a good that is the *highest good* in the world and also possible through our cooperation is a need [arising] not from a deficiency in moral incentives but from a deficieny in the external relations within which alone an object as end in itself (as moral *final end*) can be produced in conformity with these incentives. For without some end there can be no *will*, although, if it is a question only of lawful necessitation of actions, one must abstract from any end and the law alone constitutes its determining ground. But not every end is moral (e.g., that of one's own happiness is not), but this must rather be an unselfish one; and the need for a final end assigned   [280] by pure reason and comprehending the whole of all ends under one principle (a world as the highest good and possible through our cooperation) is a need of an unselfish will *extending* itself beyond observance of the formal law to production of an object (the highest good). This is a special kind of determination of the will, namely through the idea of the whole of all ends, the basis of which is that *if* we stand in certain moral relations to things in the world we must everywhere obey the moral law, and beyond this there is added the duty to bring it about as far as we can *that* such a relation (a world in keeping with the moral highest ends) exists. In this the human being thinks of himself by analogy with the Deity who, although subjectively in need of no external thing, still cannot be thought to shut himself up within himself but rather to be determined to produce the highest good beyond himself just by his consciousness of his complete self-sufficiency; and this necessity in the supreme being (which in the human being is a duty) can be represented *by us* only as a moral need. With the human being too, accordingly, the incentive which is present in the idea of the highest good possible in the world by his cooperation is not his own happiness thereby intended but only this idea as end in itself, and hence compliance with it as duty. For it contains no prospect of happiness absolutely, but only of a proportion between it and the worthiness of a subject, whatever that may be. But a determination of will which limits itself and its aim of belonging to such a whole to this condition is *not selfish*. [I.K.]

b. Garve expresses this proposition as follows: "that the virtuous person can never lose sight of that perspective (his own happiness) nor may he do so, since otherwise he would lose altogether passage into the invisible world, to conviction of the
[281] existence of God and of immortality, which is yet, according to
this theory, absolutely necessary *to give the moral system support
and stability*"; and he then concludes by briefly summing up the
assertions he attributes to me: "The virtuous person, according to
those principles, strives unceasingly to be worthy of happiness,
but never, *insofar as* he is truly virtuous, to be happy." (The words
insofar as create an ambiguity here, which must be settled at the
outset. They can mean, *in the act* by which, as virtuous he subjects
himself to his duty, in which case this proposition is perfectly in
accord with my theory. Or they can mean that just by his being
virtuous generally, and so even when it is not a matter of duty and
there would be no conflict with it, a virtuous person should still
have no regard at all for happiness; and this quite contradicts my
assertions.)

These objections are therefore nothing but misunderstandings
(for I do not care to take them as misinterpretations), and their
possibility would have to be astonishing, did not the human
propensity to follow one's accustomed course of thought even in
appraising the thoughts of others, and thus to carry the former
over into the latter, adequately explain such a phenomenon.

[284] ....

I now come to the point that really concerns us here, namely
to illustrate with examples and to test the supposed conflicting
interests of theory and of practice in philosophy. Garve gives the
best example of it in his treatise cited above. He says first (speaking of the distinction I find between a doctrine of how we are to
become *happy* and one of how we are to become *worthy* of happiness): "For my own part, I confess that I very well conceive this
division of ideas in my *head*, but that I do not find this division of
wishes in my *heart*, and that it is even inconceivable to me how
any one can become aware of having detached himself altogether
from his desire for happiness and hence aware of having performed his duty quite unselfishly."

I shall first reply to the latter. I readily grant that no one can
become aware with certainty of *having performed his duty* quite
unselfishly; for that belongs to inner experience, and to this consciousness of his state of soul there would have to belong a perfectly clear representation of all the associated representations
and considerations attached to the concept of duty by imagina-

tion, habit, and inclination, which cannot be required in any case; and, in general, the nonexistence of something (and so too of a covertly thought advantage) cannot be an object of experience. But that the human being *ought to perform* his duty quite unselfishly and that he *must* altogether separate his craving for happiness from the concept of duty, in order to have this concept quite pure: of that he is aware with the utmost clarity or, should he believe that he is not, it can be required of him that he be so, as far as he can; for the true worth of morality is to be found precisely in this purity, and he must therefore also be capable of it. Perhaps no one has ever preformed quite unselfishly (without [285] admixture of other incentives) the duty he cognizes and also reveres; perhaps no one will ever succeed in doing so, however hard he tries. But insofar as, in examining himself most carefully, he can perceive not only no such cooperating motive but instead self-denial with respect to many motives opposing the idea of duty, he can become aware of a maxim of striving for such purity; that he is capable of, and that is also sufficient for his observance of duty. On the other hand, to make it his maxim to foster the influence of such motives, on the pretext that human nature does not admit of such purity (though this, again, he cannot assert with certainty) is the death of all morality.

As for Garve's avowal, just cited, that he does not find such a division (strictly speaking, separation) in his *heart*, I have no hesitation in contradicting his self-accusation outright and in championing his heart against his head. He, a man of integrity, has actually *found* this separation in his heart every time (in his determination of will), only it would not be reconciled in his head[1]—for the sake of speculation and of comprehending what is

---

1 Professor Garve (in his notes to Cicero's book on duties [*De Officiis*], 1783 edition, p. 69) makes the following admission, notable and worthy of his acuteness: "Freedom, according to his innermost conviction, will always remain unresolved and will never be explained." A proof of its reality can absolutely not be found either in an immediate or in a mediate experience; and yet one also cannot accept it without any proof. Since a proof of its reality cannot be derived from merely theoretical grounds (for these would have to be sought in experience) and must therefore be derived from practical rational propositions only—but not from technically practical ones (since these would in turn require experiential grounds)—and can consequently be derived only from morally practical propositions, one has to wonder why Garve did not have recourse to the concept of freedom, so as at least to save the possibility of such imperatives. [I.K.]

incomprehensible (inexplicable), namely the possibility of categorical imperatives (such as those of duty are)—with the usual principles of psychological explanation (all of which have the mechanism of natural necessity as their basis).

But I must loudly and zealously contradict Garve when he concludes by saying: "Such fine distinctions among ideas already become *obscure* in *reflecting* upon particular objects; but they *disappear completely* when it comes to *acting*, when they are to be applied to desires and purposes. The more simple, rapid and *stripped of clear representations* is the step by which we pass from considering motives to actually acting, so much the less is it possible to cognize precisely and surely the determinate weight that each motive contributed to guiding the step in this and in no other way."

[286]

The concept of duty in its complete purity is not only incomparably simpler, clearer and, for practical use, more readily grasped and more natural to everyone than any motive derived from happiness, or mixed with it and with regard for it (which always requires much art and reflection); it is also, even in the judgment of the most common human reason—if only the concept is presented in its purity to a human will, separated from and even in opposition to the latter—far *more powerful*, forceful, and promising of results than all motives borrowed from the latter, selfish principle. Take the case, for example, that someone is holding in trust something belonging to another (*depositum*), the owner of which has died, and that the owner's heirs know nothing about it and can never come to know of it. We submit this case even to a child some eight or nine years old, and add that the holder of this deposit suffers at this very time (through no fault of his own) a complete reversal of his fortune and sees around him a miserable family of wife and children oppressed by want that he could relieve in a moment by appropriating this deposit; we add further that he is philanthropic and beneficent whereas those heirs are wealthy, hard-hearted and, besides, so thoroughly given to luxury and wastefulness that adding anything to their resources would be equivalent to throwing it into the sea. And we now ask whether, under such circumstances, it can be considered permissible for him to put this deposit to his own use. The one being questioned will undoubtedly answer, No! and, in place of any grounds, will be able to say only, It is *wrong!*—that is, it conflicts with duty. Nothing is clearer than this, though it is surely not clear that the trustee would be furthering his own *happiness* by giving up the deposit. For, if he expected to determine his decision in view of the latter he could, for example, think as follows: "If you give up the other's goods you have to the true owners [287] without being called upon to do so, they will presumably reward you for your honesty; or if that does not happen, you will acquire a good reputation at large, which can be very lucrative. But all this is most uncertain. Many doubts also arise about the opposite course: If you embezzle the deposit so as to get out of your depressed circumstances at one stroke, by making quick use of it you will incur suspicion as to how and by what means you had so soon bettered your circumstances; but if you put it to work slowly, your poverty will meanwhile increase so much it would come to be beyond remedy." By the maxim of happiness a will thus vacillates between its incentives as to what it should decide upon; for it looks to the outcome and this is highly uncertain; a good head is required to find a way out of the crush of arguments and counterarguments without cheating oneself in the total reckoning. On the other hand, if he asks himself what his duty is in this matter, he is not at all perplexed about what answer to give but certain on the spot what he has to do. He even feels, if the concept of duty counts for something with him, a revulsion merely at calculating the advantages he could gain by transgressing it, as if he still had a choice in the matter.

That these distinctions (which, as we have just shown, are not so fine as Garve thinks but are inscribed on the human soul in the broadest and most legible characters), as he says, *disappear altogether when it comes to acting* thus contradicts even his own experience. Admittedly, it does not contradict the experience that the *history* of maxims drawn from the one or the other principle presents; such experience proves, regrettably, that maxims for the most part flow from the latter principle (of selfishness); but it does contradict the experience, which can only be inward, that no idea so elevates the human mind and animates it even to inspiration as that of a pure moral disposition, revering duty above all else, struggling with the countless ills of life and even with its most seductive allurements and yet overcoming them (as we may rightly assume that one is capable of doing). That the human being is aware that he can do this because he ought to discloses within him a depth of divine predispositions and lets him feel, as it were, a holy awe at the greatness and sublimity of his true vocation. And if this attention were drawn to it more often and he [288] became used to ridding virtue completely of all the rich booty of advantages to be amassed through the observance of duty and to representing it in all its purity; if it became a principle of private and public instruction always to make use of this (a method of inculcating duties that has almost always been neglected), human morality would soon be better off. That historical experience up to now has still not proved the success of the doctrine of virtue may well be the fault of just the false presupposition that the incentive derived from the idea of duty in itself is much too fine for the common concept whereas the coarser incentive drawn from certain advantages to be expected, in this world or even in a future one, from compliance with the law (without regard for the law itself as the incentive) would work more powerfully on the mind, and that up to now it has been made a principle of education and homiletics to give preference to the aspiration for happiness over that which reason makes the supreme condition of this, namely the worthiness to by happy. For *precepts* as to how one can make oneself happy or at least avoid what is disadvantageous are not *commands*. They do not bind anyone absolutely; having been warned, one may choose what he thinks good, if he is prepared to suffer the consequences. He has no cause to regard as punishments such troubles as might issue from his failure to follow the advice he was given; for punishments happen only to a will that is free but contrary to the law; nature and inclination, however, cannot give laws to freedom. It is quite different with the idea of duty, someone's transgression of which, even without his considering the disadvantages to himself resulting from it, works immediately upon his mind and makes him reprehensible and punishable in his own eyes.

Here, then, is a clear proof that everything in moral philosophy that is correct for theory must also hold for practice. Everyone in his capacity as a human being, a being subjected by his own reason to certain duties, is accordingly *a man of affairs*; and since, as a man, he never outgrows the school of wisdom, he cannot with proud contempt, as someone supposedly better instructed by experience about what a human being is and what can be required of him, send the adherent of theory back to school. For [289] all this experience does not help him at all to escape the precept of theory, but at most only helps him to learn how theory could be better and more generally put to work, after one has adopted it into one's principles; but we are not speaking here of such pragmatic skill but only of principles.

Appendix D: From Immanuel Kant, Religion within the Limits of Reason Alone *(1793, 1794)*

[*Religion* develops Kant's notion of a kind of religion that neither rests on metaphysical assumptions that violate the limits of human cognition, nor undercuts morality. Though Kant explicitly endorses Christianity in *Religion,* his criticisms of the authority and dogma of the established Church led King Frederick William II to forbid Kant from writing or lecturing on religion. The following selections shed light on Kant's views on moral psychology, human nature, and good and evil.

From *Religion within the Boundaries of Mere Reason and Other Writings,* edited and translated by Allen Wood and George di Giovanni, Cambridge UP, 1998. Reprinted with the permission of Cambridge University Press.]

Book I, Section III. The Human Being is by Nature Evil　　　[6:32]

Vitiis nemo sine nascitur, Horace[1]

... [The] statement, "The human being is *evil,*" cannot mean anything else than that he is conscious of the moral law and yet has incorporated into his maxim the (occasional) deviation from it. "He is evil *by nature,*" simply means that being evil applies to him considered in his species; not that this quality may be inferred from the concept of his species ([i.e.] from the concept of the human being in general, for then the quality would be necessary), but rather that, according to the cognition we have of the human being through experience, he cannot be judged otherwise, in other words, we may presuppose evil as subjectively necessary in every human being, even the best. Now, since this propensity[2] must itself be considered morally evil, hence not a natural predisposition but something that a human being can be held accountable for, and consequently must consist in maxims of the

---

1　*Satires,* I, iii, 68. "Nobody is born without vice." [A.W., G.G.]

2　According to Kant: "*Propensity* is actually only the *predisposition* to desire an enjoyment which, when the subject has experienced it, arouses *inclination* to it" (6:29n; Wood-Giovanni translation).

power of choice[1] contrary to the law and yet, because of freedom, such maxims must be viewed as accidental, a circumstance that would not square with the universality of the evil at issue unless their supreme subjective ground were not in all cases somehow entwined with humanity itself and, as it were, rooted in it: so we can call this ground a natural propensity to evil, and, since it must nevertheless always come about through one's own fault, we can further call it a *radical* innate *evil* in human nature (not any the less brought upon us by ourselves).

....

[36]   The human being (even the worst) does not repudiate the moral law, whatever his maxims, in rebellious attitude (by revoking obedience to it). The law rather imposes itself on him irresistibly, because of his moral predisposition; and if no other incentive were at work against it, he would also incorporate it into his supreme maxim as sufficient determination of his power of choice, i.e. he would be morally good. He is, however, also dependent on the incentives of his sensuous nature because of his equally innocent natural predisposition, and he incorporates them too into his maxim (according to the subjective principle of self-love). If he took them into his maxim *as of themselves sufficient* for the determination of his power of choice, without minding the moral law (which he nonetheless has within himself), he would then become morally evil. But now, since he naturally incorporates both into the same maxim, whereas he would find each, taken alone, of itself sufficient to determine the will, so, if the difference between maxims depended simply on the difference between incentives (the material of the maxims), namely, on whether the law or the sense impulse provides the incentive, he would be morally good and evil at the same time—and this is a contradiction.... Hence the difference, whether the human being

---

1   "*Willkür*" is here translated as "power of choice." In *Religion* and other of Kant's post-*Groundwork* ethical writings, such as the *Critique of Practical Reason* and the *Metaphysics of Morals*, Kant identifies *Willkür* with the human faculty of choice, which adopts maxims; he sometimes identifies *Wille* (will) only with pure practical reason, which is the source of the moral law, but other times uses "*Wille*" to refer to the entire faculty of volition (including both the faculty of choice and pure practical reason). For more on this distinction, see Henry E. Allison, *Kant's Theory of Freedom* (Cambridge: Cambridge UP, 1990), 129-36; and Lewis White Beck, *A Commentary on Kant's Critique of Practical Reason* (Chicago: U of Chicago P, 1960), 176-81.

is good or evil, must not lie in the difference between the incentives that he incorporates into his maxim (not in the material of the maxim) but in their *subordination* (the form of the maxim): *which of the two he makes the condition of the other.* It follows that the human being (even the best) is evil only because he reverses the moral order of his incentives in incorporating them into his maxims. He indeed incorporates the moral law into those maxims, together with the law of self-love; since, however, he realizes that the two cannot stand on an equal footing, but one must be subordinated to the other as its supreme condition, he makes the incentives of self-love and their inclinations the condition of compliance with the moral law—whereas it is this latter that, as *the supreme condition* of the satisfaction of the former, should have been incorporated into the universal maxim of the power of choice as the sole incentive.

Appendix E: From Immanuel Kant, Metaphysics of Morals (1797)

[In *Metaphysics of Morals*, Kant builds on his *Groundwork for the Metaphysics of Morals* and provides a substantive, normative account of the duties human beings have to themselves and to one another. Kant divides *Metaphysics of Morals* into two parts, which were originally published separately. The "Doctrine of Right" is Kant's account of the sphere or right, or public justice. It also contains Kant's justification of private property and his theory of punishment. The "Doctrine of Virtue" sets forth Kant's general account of "directly ethical" duties to oneself and to others, and provides Kant's theory of virtue. Its account of duties is "general" because apart from a discussion of friendship, it makes no attempt to explicate duties generated by special relationships. The following excerpts are primarily from the introductions to the "Doctrine of Right" and the "Doctrine of Virtue," though they also contain some further discussions of duties to oneself and to others.

From *Kant: Practical Philosophy*, edited and translated by Mary J. Gregor, Cambridge UP, 1996. Reprinted with the permission of Cambridge University Press.]

Introduction to the Doctrine of Right [6:229]

A. What the Doctrine of Right Is.

The sum of those laws for which an external lawgiving is possible is called the *Doctrine of Right (Ius)....*

B. What Is Right?

.... [230]

The concept of right, insofar as it is related to an obligation corresponding to it (i.e., the moral concept of right), has to do, *first*, only with the external and indeed practical relation of one person to another, insofar as their actions, as deeds, can have (direct or indirect) influence on each other. But, *second*, it does not signify the relation of one's choice to the mere wish (hence also to the mere need) of the other, as in actions of beneficence or callousness, but only a relation to the other's *choice. Third*, in this reciprocal relation of choice no account at all is taken of the *matter* of choice, that is, of the end each has in mind with the object he wants; it is not asked, for example, whether someone who buys goods from me for his own commercial use will gain by the transaction or not. All that is in question is the *form* in the relation of choice on the part of both, insofar as choice is regarded merely as *free*, and whether the action of one can be united with the freedom of the other in accordance with a universal law.

Right is therefore the sum of the conditions under which the choice of one can be united with the choice of another in accordance with a universal law of freedom.

C. The Universal Principle of Right.

"Any action is *right* if it can coexist with everyone's freedom in accordance with a universal law, or if on its maxim the freedom of choice of each can coexist with everyone's freedom in accordance with a universal law."

[231] If then my action or my condition generally can coexist with the freedom of everyone in accordance with a universal law, whoever hinders me in it does me *wrong*; for this hindrance (resistance) cannot coexist with freedom in accordance with a universal law.

It also follows from this that it cannot be required that this principle of all maxims be itself in turn my maxim, that is, it cannot be required that *I make it the maxim* of my action; for anyone can be free so long as I do not impair his freedom by my *external action*, even though I am quite indifferent to his freedom or would like in my heart to infringe upon it. That I make it my maxim to act rightly is a demand that ethics makes on me.

Thus the universal law of right, so act externally that the free use of your choice can coexist with the freedom of everyone in accordance with a universal law, is indeed a law that lays an obligation on me, but it does not at all expect, far less demand, that I *myself should* limit my freedom to those conditions just for the sake of this obligation; instead, reason says only that freedom *is* limited to those conditions in conformity with the idea of it and that it may also be actively limited by others; and it says this as a postulate that is incapable of further proof.—When one's aim is not to teach virtue but only to set forth what is *right*, one need not and should not represent that law of right as itself the incentive to action.

D. Right Is Connected with an Authorization to Use Coercion.

Resistance that counteracts the hindering of an effect promotes this effect and is consistent with it. Now whatever is wrong is a hindrance to freedom in accordance with universal laws. But coercion is a hindrance or resistance to freedom. Therefore, if a certain use of freedom is itself a hindrance to freedom in accordance with universal laws (i.e., wrong), coercion that is opposed to this (as a *hindering of a hindrance to freedom*) is consistent with freedom in accordance with universal laws, that is, it is right. Hence there is connected with right by the principle of contradiction an authorization to coerce someone who infringes upon it.

....

Division of the Doctrine of Right   [236]

A. General division of duties of right.

One can follow Ulpian[1] in making this division if a sense is ascribed to his formulae which he may not have thought distinctly in them but which can be explicated from them or put into them. They are the following:
1) *Be an honorable human being* (*honeste vive*). *Rightful honor* (*honestas iuridica*) consists in asserting one's worth as a human being in relation to others, a duty expressed by the saying, "Do not make yourself a mere means for others but be at the same time an end for them." This duty will be explained later as obligation from the right of humanity in our own person (*Lex iusti*).
2) *Do not wrong anyone* (*neminem laede*) even if, to avoid doing so, you should have to stop associating with others and shun all society (*Lex iuridica*).
3) (If you cannot help associating with others), *enter* into a society with them in which each can keep what is his (*suum cuique tribue*).—If this last formula were translated "Give to each what is his," what it says would be absurd, since one cannot give anyone something he already has. In order to make sense it would have to read: "*Enter* a condition in which what belongs to each can be secured to him against everyone else" (*Lex iustitiae*).   [237]

---

1 The prolific Roman jurist Domitius Ulpianus (d. 288).

So the above three classical formulae serve also as principles for dividing the system of duties of right into *internal* duties, *external* duties, and duties that involve the derivation of the latter from the principle of the former by subsumption.

B. General division of rights.

1. As systematic *doctrines*, rights are divided into *natural right*, which rests only on a priori principles, and *positive* (statutory) right, which proceeds from the will of a legislator.
2. The highest division of rights, as (moral) *capacities* for putting others under obligations (i.e., as a lawful basis, *titulum*, for doing so), is the division into *innate* and *acquired* right. An innate right is that which belongs to everyone by nature, independently of any act that would establish a right; an acquired right is that for which such an act is required.

What is innately mine or yours can also be called what is internally mine or yours (*meum vel tuum internum*); for what is externally mine or yours must always be acquired.

There is only one innate right.

Freedom (independence from being constrained by another's choice), insofar as it can coexist with the freedom of every other in accordance with a universal law, is the only original right belonging to every man by virtue of his humanity.—This principle of innate freedom already involves the following authorizations, which are not really distinct from it (as if they were members of the division of some higher concept of a right): innate *equality*, that is, independence from being bound by others to more than one can in turn bind them; hence a [238] human being's quality of being *his own master* (*sui iuris*), as well as being a human being *beyond reproach* (*iusti*), since before he performs any act affecting rights he has done no wrong to anyone; and finally, his being authorized to do to others anything that does not in itself diminish what is theirs, so long as they do not want to accept it—such things as merely communicating his thoughts to them, telling or promising them something, whether what he says is true and sincere or untrue and insincere (*veriloquium aut falsiloquium*);

for it is entirely up to them whether they want to believe him or not.[1]

The aim in introducing such a division within the system of natural right (insofar as it is concerned with innate right) is that when a dispute arises about an acquired right and the question comes up, on whom does the burden of proof (*onus probandi*) fall, either about a controversial fact or, if this is settled, about a controversial right, someone who refuses to accept this obligation can appeal methodically to his innate right to freedom (which is now specified in its various relations), as if he were appealing to various bases of rights.

With regard to what is innately, hence internally, mine or yours, there are not several *rights*; there is only *one* right. Since this highest division consists of two members very unequal in content, it can be put in the prolegomena and the division of the doctrine of right can refer only to what is externally mine or yours.

....

Introduction to the Doctrine of Virtue [379]

I. Discussion of the Concept of a Doctrine of Virtue.

The very *concept of duty* is already the concept of a *necessitation* (constraint) of free choice through the law. This constraint may be an *external constraint* or a *self-constraint*. The moral *imperative*

---

1 Telling an untruth intentionally, even though merely frivolously, is usually called a lie (*mendacium*) because it can also harm someone, at least to the extent that if he ingenuously repeats it others ridicule him as gullible. The only kind of untruth we want to call a lie, in the sense *bearing upon rights*, is one that directly infringes upon another's right, e.g., the false allegation that a contract has been concluded with someone, made in order to deprive him of what is his (*falsiloquium dolosum*). And this distinction between closely related concepts is not without basis; for when someone merely says what he thinks, another always remains free to take it as he pleases. But a rumor, having some basis, that this is a human being whose talk cannot be believed comes so close to the reproach of calling him a liar that the borderline separating what belongs to *Ius* from what must be assigned to ethics can only be drawn in just this way. [I.K.]

makes this constraint known through the categorical nature of its pronouncement (the unconditional ought.) Such constraint, therefore, does not apply to rational beings as such (there could also be *holy* ones) but rather to *human beings*, rational *natural* beings, who are unholy enough that pleasure can induce them to break the moral law, even though they recognize its authority; and even when they do obey the law, they do it *reluctantly* (in the face of opposition from their inclinations), and it is in this that such [380] *constraint* properly consists.[1]—But since the human being is still a *free* (moral) being, when the concept of duty concerns the internal determination of his will (the incentive) the constraint that the concept of duty contains can be only self-constraint (through the representation of the law alone); for only so can that *necessitation* (even if it is external) be united with the freedom of his choice. Hence in this case the concept of duty will be an ethical one.

Impulses of nature, accordingly, involve *obstacles* within the human being's mind to his fulfillment of duty and (sometimes powerful) forces opposing it, which he must judge that he is capable of resisting and conquering by reason not at some time in the future but at once (the moment he thinks of duty): he must judge that he *can* do what the law tells him unconditionally that he *ought* to do.

Now the capacity and considered resolve to withstand a strong but unjust opponent is *fortitude* (*fortitudo*) and, with respect to what opposes the moral disposition *within us*, **virtue** (*virtus, fortitudo moralis*). So the part of the general doctrine of duties that brings inner, rather than outer, freedom under laws is a *doctrine of virtue*.

---

1 Yet if a human being looks at himself objectively (under the aspect of *humanity* in his own person), as his pure practical reason determines him to do, he finds that *as a moral being* he is also holy enough to break the inner law *reluctantly*; for there is no human being so depraved as not to feel an opposition to breaking it and an abhorrence of himself in the face of which he has to constrain himself [to break the law].—Now it is impossible to explain the phenomenon that at this parting of the ways (where the beautiful fable places Hercules between virtue and sensual pleasure) the human being shows more propensity to listen to his inclinations than to the law. For we can explain what happens only by deriving it from a cause in accordance with laws of nature, and in so doing we would not be thinking of choice as free.—But it is this self-constraint in opposite directions and its unavoidability that makes known the inexplicable property of *freedom* itself. [I.K.]

The doctrine of right dealt only with the *formal* condition of outer freedom (the consistency of outer freedom with itself if its maxims were made universal law), that is, with **right**. But ethics goes beyond this and provides a *matter* (an object of free choice), an **end** of pure reason which it represents as an end that is also objectively necessary, that is, an end that, as far as human beings are concerned, it is a duty to have.—For since the sensible inclinations of human beings tempt them to ends (the matter of choice) that can be contrary to duty, lawgiving reason can in turn [381] check their influence only by a moral end set up against the ends of inclination, an end that must therefore be given a priori, independently of inclinations.

An *end* is an object of the choice (of a rational being), through the representation of which choice is determined to an action to bring this object about.—Now, I can indeed be constrained by others to perform *actions* that are directed as means to an end, but I can never be constrained by others *to have an end*: only I myself can *make* something my end.—But if I am under obligation to make my end something that lies in concepts of practical reason, and so to have, besides the formal determining ground of choice (such as right contains), a material one as well, an end that could be set against the end arising from sensible impulses, this would be the concept of an *end that is in itself a duty*. But the doctrine of this end would not belong to the doctrine of right but rather to ethics, since *self-constraint* in accordance with (moral) laws belongs to the concept of ethics alone.

For this reason ethics can also be defined as the system of the *ends* of pure practical reason.—Ends and duties distinguish the two divisions of the doctrine of morals in general. That ethics contains duties that one cannot be constrained by others (through natural means) to fulfill follows merely from its being a doctrine of *ends*, since *coercion* to ends (to have them) is self-contradictory.

That ethics is a *doctrine of virtue* (*doctrina officiorum virtutis*) follows, however, from the above exposition of virtue when it is connected with the kind of obligation whose distinctive feature was just pointed out.—That is to say, determination to an *end* is the only determination of choice the very concept of which excludes the possibility of constraint *through natural means* by the *choice* of another. Another can indeed *coerce* me *to do* something that is not my end (but only a means to another's end), but not to *make this my end*; and yet I can have no end without making it

an end for myself. To have an end that I have not myself made an end is self-contradictory, an act of freedom which is yet not free.—But it is no contradiction to set an end for myself that is [382] also a duty, since I constrain myself to it and this is altogether consistent with freedom.[1]—But how is such an end possible? That is the question now. For that the concept of a thing is possible (not self-contradictory) is not yet sufficient for assuming the possibility of the thing itself (the objective reality of the concept).
....

VI. Ethics Does Not Give Laws for *Actions* (*Ius* Does That), But Only for *Maxims* of Actions.

The concept of duty stands in immediate relation to a *law* (even [389] if I abstract from all ends, as the matter of the law). The formal principle of duty, in the categorical imperative "So act that the maxim of your action could become a universal *law*," already indicates this. Ethics adds only that this principle is to be thought as the law of *your* own will and not of will in general, which could also be the will of others; in the later case the law would provide a duty of right, which lies outside the sphere of ethics.—Maxims are here regarded as subjective principles which merely *qualify* for a giving of universal law, and the requirement that they so qualify is only a negative principle (not to come into conflict with a law as such).—How can there be, beyond this principle, a law for the maxims of actions?

Only the concept of an *end* that is also a duty, a concept that belongs exclusively to ethics, establishes a law for maxims of actions by subordinating the subjective end (that everyone has) to the objective end (that everyone ought to make his end). The imperative "You ought to make this or that (e.g., the happiness of others) your end" has to do with the matter of choice (an object).

---

1 The less a human being can be constrained by natural means and the more he can be constrained morally (through the mere representation of duty), so much the more free he is. Suppose, for example, one so firm of purpose and strong of soul that he cannot be dissuaded from a pleasure he intends to have, no matter how others may reason with him about the harm he will do himself by it. If such a one gives up his plan immediately, though reluctantly, at the thought that by carrying it out he would omit one of his duties as an official or neglect a sick father, he proves his freedom in the highest degree by being unable to resist the call of duty. [I.K.]

Now, no free action is possible unless the agent also intends an end (which is the matter of choice). Hence, if there is an end that is also a duty, the only condition that maxims of actions, as means to ends, must contain is that of qualifying for a possible giving of universal law. On the other hand, the end that is also a duty can make it a law to have such a maxim, although for the maxim itself the mere possibility of agreeing with a giving of universal law is already sufficient.

For maxims of actions can be *arbitrary*, and are subject only to the limiting condition of being fit for a giving of universal law, which is the formal principle of actions. A *law*, however, takes arbitrariness away from actions, and this distinguishes it from any *recommendation* (where all that one requires is to know the most suitable means to an end).

VII. Ethical Duties Are of *Wide* Obligation, Whereas Duties of [390] Right Are of *Narrow* Obligation.

This proposition follows from the preceding one; for if the law can prescribe only the maxim of actions, not actions themselves, this is a sign that it leaves a playroom (*latitudo*) for free choice in following (complying with) the law, that is, that the law cannot specify precisely in what way one is to act and how much one is to do by the action for an end that is also a duty.—But a wide duty is not to be taken as permission to make exceptions to the maxim of actions but only as permission to limit one maxim of duty by another (e.g., love of one's neighbor in general by love of one's parents), by which in fact the field for the practice of virtue is widened.—The wider the duty, therefore, the more imperfect is a man's obligation to action; as he, nevertheless, brings closer to *narrow* duty (duties of right) the maxim of complying with wide duty (in his disposition), so much the more perfect is his virtuous action.

Imperfect duties alone are, accordingly, *duties of virtue.*[1] Fulfillment of them is *merit (meritum)* = +a; but failure to fulfill them is not in itself *culpability (demeritum)* = −a but rather mere *deficiency in moral worth* (= 0), unless the subject should make it his principle not to comply with such duties. It is only the strength of

---

1 Or, according to a previous Gregor translation, "imperfect duties are, accordingly, only duties of virtue" (*The Metaphysics of Morals* [Cambridge: Cambridge UP, 1991], 194).

one's resolution, in the first case, that is properly called *virtue* (*virtus*); one's weakness, in the second case, is not so much *vice* (*vitium*) as rather mere *want of virtue*, lack of moral strength (*defectus moralis*). (As the word "*Tugend*" [virtue]comes from "*taugen*" [to be fit for]so "*Untugend*" [lack of virtue]comes from "*zu nichts taugen*" [not to be fit for anything].) Every action contrary to duty is called a *transgression* (*peccatum*). It is when an intentional trasngression has become a principle that it is properly called a *vice* (*vitium*).

Although there is nothing meritorious in the conformity of one's actions with right (in being an honest human being), the conformity with right of one's maxims of such actions, as duties, that is, **respect** for right, is *meritorious*. For one thereby *makes* the right of humanity, or also the right of human beings, one's *end*

[391] and in so doing widens one's concept of duty beyond the concept of what is *due* (*officium debiti*), since another can indeed by his right require of me actions in accordance with the law, but not that the law be also my incentive to such actions. The same holds true of the universal ethical command, "act in conformity with duty *from* duty." To establish and quicken this disposition in oneself is, as in the previous case, *meritorious*, since it goes beyond the law of duty for actions and makes the law itself also the incentive.

But for this very reason these duties, too, must be counted as duties of wide obligation. With respect to them (and indeed, in order to bring wide obligation as close as possible to the concept of narrow obligation), there is a subjective principle of ethical *reward*, that is, a receptivity to being rewarded in accordance with laws of virtue: the reward, namely, of a moral pleasure that goes beyond mere contentment with onself (which can be merely negative) and which is celebrated in the saying that, through consciousness of this pleasure, virtue is its own reward.

If this merit is a human being's merit in relation to other human beings for promoting what all human beings recognize as their natural end (for making their happiness his own), it could be called *sweet merit*; for consciousness of it produces a moral enjoyment in which men are inclined by sympathy *to revel*. But *bitter merit*, which comes from promoting the true well-being of others even when they fail to recognize it as such (when they are unappreciative and ungrateful), usually yields no such return. All that it produces is *contentment* with oneself, although in this case the merit would be greater still.

VIII. Exposition of Duties of Virtue as Wide Duties.

1. One's own perfection as an end that is also a duty.

a) *Natural* perfection is the *cultivation* of any *capacities* whatever for furthering ends set forth by reason. That this is a duty and so in itself an end, and that the cultivation of our capacities, even without regard for the advantage it affords us, is based on an unconditional (moral) imperative rather than a conditional (prag- [392] matic) one, can be shown in this way. The capacity to set oneself an end—any end whatsoever—is what characterizes humanity (as distinguished from animality). Hence there is also bound up with the end of humanity in our own person the rational will, and so the duty, to make ourselves worthy of humanity by culture in general, by procuring or promoting the *capacity* to realize all sorts of possible ends, so far as this is to be found in the human being himself. In other words, the human being has a duty to cultivate the crude predispositions of his nature, by which the animal is first raised into the human being. It is therefore a duty in itself.

But this duty is a merely ethical one, that is, a duty of wide obligation. No rational principle prescribes specifically *how* far one should go in cultivating one's capacities (in enlarging or correcting one's capacity for understanding, i.e., in acquiring knowledge or skill). Then too, the different situations in which human beings may find themselves make a human being's choice of the occupation for which he should cultivate his talents very much a matter for him to decide as he chooses.—With regard to natural perfection, accordingly, there is no law of reason for actions but only a law for maxims of actions, which runs as follows: "Cultivate your powers of mind and body so that they are fit to realize any ends you might encounter," however uncertain you are which of them could sometime become yours.

b) The *cultivation of morality* in us. The greatest perfection of a human being is to do his duty *from duty* (for the law to be not only the rule but also the incentive of his actions).—At first sight this looks like a *narrow* obligation, and the principle of duty seems to prescribe with the precision and strictness of a law not only the *legality* but also the *morality* of every action, that is, the disposition. But in fact the law, here again, prescribes only the *maxim of the action*, that of seeking the basis of obligation solely in the law and not in sensible impulse (advantage or disadvantage), and hence not the *action itself.*—For a human being cannot see into the depths of his own heart so as to be quite certain, in even a *single* action, of the purity of his moral intention and the sincerity of his disposition, even when he has no doubt about the legality of the action. Very often he mistakes his own weakness, which counsels him against the venture of a misdeed, for virtue (which is the concept of strength); and how many people who have lived long [393] and guiltless lives may not be merely *fortunate* in having escaped so many temptations? In the case of any deed it remains hidden from the agent himself how much pure moral content there has been in his disposition.

Hence this duty too—the duty of assessing the worth of one's actions not by their legality alone but also by their morality (one's disposition)—is of only *wide* obligation. The law does not prescribe this inner action in the human mind but only the maxim of the action, to strive with all one's might that the thought of duty for its own sake is the sufficient incentive of every action conforming to duty.

2. The happiness of others as an end that is also a duty.

a) *Natural welfare. Benevolence* can be unlimited, since nothing need be done with it. But it is more difficult to *do good*, especially if it is to be done not from affection (love) for others but from duty, at the cost of forgoing the satisfaction of concupiscence and of active injury to it in many cases.—The reason that it is a duty to be beneficent is this: since our self-love cannot be separated from our need to be loved (helped in case of need) by others as well, we therefore make ourselves an end for others; and the only way this maxim can be binding is through its qualification as a universal law, hence through our will to make others our ends as well. The happiness of others is therefore an end that is also a duty.

But I ought to sacrifice a part of my welfare to others without hope of return, because this is a duty, and it is impossible to assign determinate limits to the extent of this sacrifice. How far it should extend depends, in large part, on what each person's true needs are in view of his sensibilities, and it must be left to each to decide this for himself. For, a maxim of promoting others' happiness at the sacrifice of one's own happiness, one's true needs, would conflict with itself if it were made a universal law. Hence this duty is only a *wide* one; the duty has in it a latitude for doing more or less, and no specific limits can be assigned to what should be done.—The law holds only for maxims, not for determinate actions.

b) The happiness of others also includes their *moral well-being* [394] (*salubritas moralis*), and we have a duty, but only a negative one, to promote this. Although the *pain* one feels from the pangs of conscience has a moral source it is still a natural effect, like grief, fear, or any other state of suffering. To see to it that another does not deservedly suffer this inner reproach is not *my* duty but *his affair*; but it is my duty to refrain from doing anything that, considering the nature of a human being, could tempt him to do something for which his conscience could afterwards pain him, to refrain from what is called giving scandal.—But this concern for others' moral contentment does not admit of determinate limits being assigned to it, so that the obligation resting on it is only a wide one.

IX. What is a Duty of Virtue?

Virtue is the strength of a human being's maxims in fulfilling his duty.—Strength of any kind can be recognized only by the obstacles it can overcome, and in the case of virtue these obstacles are natural inclinations, which can come into conflict with the human being's moral resolution; and since it is the human being *himself* who puts these obstacles in the way of his maxims, virtue is not merely a self-constraint (for then one natural inclination could strive to overcome another), but also a self-constraint in accordance with a principle of inner freedom, and so through the mere representation of one's duty in accordance with its formal law.

All duties involve a concept of *constraint* through a law. *Ethical* duties involve a constraint for which only internal lawgiving is possible, whereas duties of right involve a constraint for which external lawgiving is also possible. Both, therefore, involve constraint whether it be self-constraint or constraint by another. Since the moral capacity to constrain oneself can be called virtue, action springing from such a disposition (respect for law) can be called virtuous (ethical) action, even though the law lays down a duty of right; for it is the *doctrine of virtue* that commands us to hold the right of human beings sacred.

But what it is virtuous to do is not necessarily a *duty of virtue* strictly speaking. What it is virtuous to do may concern only *what is formal* in maxims, whereas a duty of virtue has to do with their matter, that is to say, with an end that is thought as also a duty.— [395]

But since ethical obligation to ends, of which there can be several, is only *wide* obligation—because it involves a law only for *maxims* of actions, and an end is the matter (object) of choice—there are many different duties, corresponding to the different ends prescribed by the law, which are called *duties of virtue (officia honestatis)* just because they are subject only to free constraint, not constraint by other human beings, and because they determine an end that is also a duty.

Like anything *formal*, virtue as the will's conformity with every duty, based on a firm disposition, is merely one and the same. But with respect to the *end* of actions that is also a duty, that is, what one *ought* to make one's *end* (what is material), there can be several virtues; and since obligation to the maxim of such an end is called a duty of virtue, there are many duties of virtue.

The supreme principle of the doctrine of virtue is: act in accordance with a maxim of *ends* that it can be a universal law for everyone to have.—In accordance with this principle a human being is an end for himself as well as for others, and it is not enough that he is not authorized to use either himself or others merely as means (since he could then still be indifferent to them); it is in itself his duty to make the human being as such his end.

This basic principle of the doctrine of virtue, as a categorical imperative, cannot be proved, but it can be given a deduction from pure practical reason.—What, in the relation of a human being to himself and others, *can* be an end *is* an end for pure practical reason; for, pure practical reason is a faculty of ends generally, and for it to be indifferent to ends, that is, to take no interest in them, would therefore be a contradiction, since then it would not determine maxims for actions either (because every maxim of action contains an end) and so would not be practical reason. But pure reason can prescribe no ends a priori without setting them forth as also duties, and such duties are then called duties of virtue.

....

Doctrine of the Elements of Ethics, Part I, On Duties to Oneself as Such, Introduction

[418]   §4. On the principle on which the division of duties to oneself is based.

[419]   The division can be made only with regard to objects of duty, not with regard to the subject that puts himself under obligation. The

subject that is bound, as well as the subject that binds, is always the *human being only*; and though we may, in a theoretical respect, distinguish soul and body from each other, as natural characteristics of a human being, we may not think of them as different substances putting him under obligation, so as to justify a division of duties to the *body* and duties to the *soul*.—Neither experience nor inferences of reason give us adequate grounds for deciding whether the human being has a soul (in the sense of a substance dwelling in him, distinct from the body and capable of thinking independently of it, that is, a spiritual substance), or whether life may not well be, instead, a property of matter. And even if the first alternative be true, it is still inconceivable that he should have a duty to a *body* (as a subject imposing obligation), even to a human body.

1) The only *objective* division of duties to oneself will, accordingly, be the division into what is **formal** and what is **material** in duties to oneself. The first of these are *limiting* (negative) duties; the second, *widening* (positive duties to oneself). Negative duties *forbid* a human being to act contrary to the **end** of his nature and so have to do merely with his moral *self-preservation*; positive duties, which *command* him to make a certain object of choice his end, concern his *perfecting* of himself. Both of them belong to virtue, either as duties of omission (*sustine et abstine*) or as duties of commission (*viribus consessis utere*), but both belong to it as duties of virtue. The first belong to the moral **health** (*ad esse*) of a human being as object of both his outer senses and his inner sense, to the *preservation* of his nature in its perfection (as *receptivity*). The second belong to his moral *prosperity* (*ad melius esse, opulentia moralis*), which consists in possessing a *capacity* sufficient for all his ends, insofar as this can be acquired; they belong to his *cultivation* (active perfecting) of himself.—The first principle of duty to oneself lies in the dictum "live in conformity with nature" (*naturae convenienter vive*), that is, *preserve* yourself in the perfection of your nature; the second, in the saying "*make yourself more perfect* than mere nature has made you" (*perfice te ut finem, perfice te ut medium*).[1]

2) There will be a *subjective* division of a human being's duties to himself, that is, one in terms of whether the subject of duty [420]

---

1 This translates to, "perfect yourself as an end, perfect yourself as a means."

(the human being) views himself both as an **animal** (natural) and moral being or **only as a moral** being.

There are impulses of nature having to do with man's **animality**. Through them nature aims at a) his self-preservation, b) the preservation of the species, and c) the preservation of his capacity to enjoy life, though still on the animal level only.—The vices that are opposed to his duty to himself are *murdering himself*, the unnatural use of his *sexual inclination*, and such *excessive consumption of food and drink* as weakens his capacity for making purposive use of his powers.[1]

But a human being's duty to himself as a moral being *only* (without taking his animality into consideration) consists in what is *formal* in the consistency of the maxims of the will with the *dignity* of humanity in his person. It consists, therefore, in the prohibition against depriving himself of the *prerogative* of a moral being, that of acting in accordance with principles, that is, inner freedom, and so making himself a plaything of the mere inclinations and hence a thing.—The vices contrary to this duty are **lying, avarice**, and **false humility** (servility). These adopt principles that are directly contrary to his character as a moral being (in terms of its very form), that is, to inner freedom, the innate dignity of a human being, which is tantamount to saying that they make it one's basic principle to have no basic principle and hence no character, that is, to throw oneself away and make oneself an object of contempt.— The virtue that is opposed to all these vices could be called *love of honor* (*honestas interna, iustum sui aestimium*), a cast of mind far removed from *ambition* (*ambitio*) (which can be quite mean)....

[421] **Doctrine of the Elements of Ethics, Part I, Book 1, Chapter 1, On perfect duties to onself as an animal and moral being**

Article 1, "On killing oneself."

[422] Killing oneself is a crime (murder). It can also be regarded as a violation of one's duty to other people (the duty of spouses to each other, of parents to their children, of a subject to his superior or to his fellow citizens, and finally even as a violation of duty to God, as his abandoning the post assigned him in the world

---

1 That is, we have duties to ourselves as animal and moral beings to avoid maxims that instantiate the vices of suicide and self-mutilation, sexual self-degradation, and gluttony and drunkenness.

without having been called away from it). But since what is in question here is only a violation of duty to oneself, the question is whether, if I set aside all those relations, a human being is still bound to preserve his life simply by virtue of his quality as a person and whether he must acknowledge in this a duty (and indeed a strict duty) to himself.

It seems absurd to say that a human being could wrong himself (*volenti non fit iniuria*).[1] Hence the Stoic thought it a prerogative of his (the sage's) personality to depart from life at his discretion (as from a smoke-filled room) with peace of soul, free from the pressure of present or anticipated ills, because he could be of no more use in life.—But there should have been in this very courage, this strength of soul not to fear death and to know of something that the human being can value even more highly than his life, a still stronger motive for him not to destroy himself, a being with such powerful authority over the strongest sensible incentives, and so not to deprive himself of life.

A human being cannot renounce his personality as long as he is a subject of duty, hence as long as he lives; and it is a contradiction that he should be authorized to withdraw from all obligation, that is, freely to act as if no authorization were needed for this action. To annihilate the subject of morality in one's own person [423] is to root out the existence of morality itself from the world, as far as one can, even though morality is an end in itself. Consequently, disposing of oneself as a mere means to some discretionary end is debasing humanity in one's own person (*homo noumenon*),[2] to which the human being (*homo phaenomenon*)[3] was nevertheless entrusted for preservation.

To deprive oneself of an integral part or organ (to maim oneself)—for example, to give away or sell a tooth to be transplanted into another's mouth, or to have oneself castrated in order to get an easier livelihood as a singer, and so forth—are ways of partially murdering oneself. But to have a dead or diseased organ amputated when it endangers one's life, or to have something cut off that is a part but not an organ of the body, for example, one's hair, cannot be counted as a crime against one's own person—

1   "No one is wronged willingly." [M.J.G.]
2   "*Homo noumenon*" refers to the human being thought of only in terms of his personality or inner freedom, that is, as a rational being who legislates the moral law and can act morally for its own sake.
3   "*Homo phaenomenon*" refers to the embodied human being, who is rational but who is also part of the deterministic, sensible world.

although cutting one's hair in order to sell it is not altogether free from blame.

Casuistical questions.

Is it murdering oneself to hurl oneself to certain death (like Curtius)[1] in order to save one's country?—or is deliberate martyrdom, sacrificing oneself for the good of all humanity, also to be considered an act of heroism?

Is it permitted to anticipate by killing oneself the unjust death sentence of one's ruler—even if the ruler permits this (as did Nero with Seneca)? Can a great king who died recently[2] be charged with a criminal intention for carrying a fast-acting poison with him, presumably so that if he were captured when he led his troops into battle he could not be forced to agree to conditions of ransom harmful to his state?—for one can ascribe this purpose to him without having to presume that mere pride lay behind it.

[424] A man who had been bitten by a mad dog already felt hydrophobia coming on. He explained, in a letter he left, that, since as far as he knew the disease was incurable, he was taking his life lest he harm others as well in his madness (the onset of which he already felt). Did he do wrong?

Anyone who decides to be vaccinated against smallpox puts his life in danger, even though he does it *in order to preserve his life*; and, insofar as he himself brings on the disease that endangers his life, he is in a far more doubtful situation, as far as the law of duty is concerned, than is the sailor, who at least does not arouse the storm to which he entrusts himself. Is smallpox inoculation, then, permitted?...

[From the episodic section, "On an **amphiboly** in **moral concepts of reflection**, taking what is a human being's duty to himself for a duty to other beings."]

§17.

[443] A propensity to wanton destruction of what is *beautiful* in inanimate nature (*spiritus destructionis*) is opposed to a human being's duty to himself; for it weakens or uproots that feeling in him which, though not of itself moral, is still a disposition of sensibil-

---

1 Legendary Roman hero Marcus Curtius.
2 Frederick the Great. [M.J.G.]

ity that greatly promotes morality or at least prepares the way for it: the disposition, namely, to love something (e.g., beautiful crystal formations, the indescribable beauty of plants) even apart from any intention to use it.

With regard to the animate but nonrational part of creation, violent and cruel treatment of animals is far more intimately opposed to a human being's duty to himself, and he has a duty to refrain from this; for it dulls his shared feeling of their suffering and so weakens and gradually uproots a natural predisposition that is very serviceable to morality in one's relations with other people. The human being is authorized to kill animals quickly (without pain) and to put them to work that does not strain them beyond their capacities (such work as he himself must submit to). But agonizing physical experiments for the sake of mere speculation, when the end could also be achieved without these, are to be abhorred.—Even gratitude for the long service of an old horse or dog (just as if they were members of the household) belongs *indirectly* to a human being's duty *with regard to* these animals; considered as a *direct* duty, however, it is always only a duty of the human being *to* himself.

....

Doctrine of the Elements of Ethics, Part II, Duties of [448]
Virtue to Others, Chapter I, On duties to others merely as
human beings

Section I. On the duty of love to other human beings.

Division.

§23.

The chief division can be that into duties to others by performing which you also put others under obligation and duties to others the observance of which does not result in obligation on the part of others.—Performing the first is *meritorious* (in relation to others); but performing the second is fulfilling a duty *that is owed.*— *Love* and *respect* are the feelings that accompany the carrying out of these duties. They can be considered separately (each by itself) and can also exist separately (one can *love* one's neighbor though he might deserve but little *respect*, and can show him the respect necessary for every human being regardless of the fact that he would hardly be judged worthy of love). But they are basically always united by the law into one duty, only in such a way that now one duty and now the other is the subject's principle, with

the other joined to it as accessory.—So we shall acknowledge that we are under obligation to help someone poor; but since the favor we do implies that his well-being depends on our generosity, and this humbles him, it is our duty to behave as if our help is either [449] merely what is due him or but a slight service of love, and to spare him humiliation and maintain his respect for himself.
....

§25.

In this context, however, **love** is not to be understood as *feeling*, that is, as pleasure in the perfection of others; love is not to be understood as *delight* in them (since others cannot put one under obligation to have feelings). It must rather be thought as the maxim of *benevolence* (practical love), which results in beneficence.

The same holds true of the **respect** to be shown to others. It is not to be understood as the mere *feeling* that comes from comparing our own *worth* with another's (such as a child feels merely from habit toward his parents, a pupil toward his teacher, or any subordinate toward his superior). It is rather to be understood as the *maxim* of limiting our self-esteem by the dignity of humanity in another person, and so as respect in the practical sense (*observantia aliis praestanda*).

Moreover, a duty of free respect toward others is, strictly speaking, only a negative one (of not exalting oneself above others) and is thus analogous to the duty of right not to encroach upon what belongs to anyone. Hence, although it is a mere duty [450] of virtue, it is regarded as *narrow* in comparison with a duty of love, and it is the latter that is considered a *wide* duty.

The duty of love for one's neighbor can, accordingly, also be expressed as the duty to make others' *ends* my own (provided only that these are not immoral). The duty of respect for my neighbor is contained in the maxim not to degrade any other to a mere means to my ends (not to demand that another throw himself away in order to slave for my end).

By carrying out the duty of love to someone I put another under obligation; I make myself deserving from him. But in observing a duty of respect I put only myself under obligation; I keep myself within my own bounds so as not to detract anything from the worth that the other, as a human being, is authorized to put upon himself.
....

[From "Division of duties of love: Sympathetic feeling is generally a duty."]

§35.
But while it is not in itself a duty to share the sufferings (as well as the joys) of others, it is a duty to sympathize actively in their fate; and to this end it is therefore an indirect duty to cultivate the compassionate natural (aesthetic) feelings in us, and to make use of them as so many means to sympathy based on moral principles and the feeling appropriate to them.—It is therefore a duty not to avoid the places where the poor who lack the most basic necessities are to be found but rather to seek them out, and not to shun sickrooms or debtors' prisons and so forth in order to avoid sharing painful feelings one may not be able to resist. For this is still one of the impulses that nature has implanted in us to do what the representation of duty alone might not accomplish.[1]
....

Section II. On duties of virtue toward other human beings aris- [462]
ing from the **respect** due them.

§38.
Every human being has a legitimate claim to respect from his fellow human beings and is *in turn* bound to respect every other. Humanity itself is a dignity; for a human being cannot be used merely as a means by any human being (either by others or even by himself) but must always be used at the same time as an end. It is just in this that his dignity (personality) consists, by which he raises himself above all other beings in the world that are not human beings and yet can be used, and so over all *things*. But just as he cannot give himself away for any price (this would conflict with his duty of self-esteem), so neither can he act contrary to the equally necessary self-esteem of others, as human beings, that is, he is under obligation to acknowledge, in a practical way, the dignity of humanity in every other human being. Hence there rests on him a duty regarding the respect that must be shown to every other human being.[2]

---

1 In addition to sympathy, duties of love include beneficence and gratitude; the vices contrary to duties of love are envy, malice, and ingratitude.
2 Duties of respect require us to reject maxims of arrogance, defamation, and ridicule.

Appendix F: From a Letter from Johann Gottlieb Fichte to Karl Leonhard Reinhold (1795)

[Johann Gottlieb Fichte (1762-1814) was heavily influenced by Kant's work. Indeed, Fichte's first work, *Attempt at a Critique of All Revelation* (1792), when its first copies appeared without an author's name, was thought by many to have been written by Kant. (Kant had been impressed by the manuscript and had helped Fichte to get it published.) Fichte's works include the *Science of Knowledge* (1795), the *Foundation of Natural Right* (1796), the *System of the Doctrine of Ethics* (1798), and the *Vocation of Man* (1800). Fichte saw much of his work in moral and political philosophy as improving on Kant's system, both by providing firmer foundations and by developing it in more compelling ways. Thus, though deeply indebted to and admiring of Kant, Fichte was also a critic. The following brief criticisms of Kant's categorical imperative are from an August 29, 1795 letter to Karl Leonhard Reinhold (1758-1823), an early promoter of Kant's philosophy, who later came to favor Fichte's thought over Kant's.

Reprinted from Johann Gottlieb Fichte, edited and translated by Daniel Breazeale, *Fichte: Early Philosophical Writings*. Copyright 1988 by Cornell University Press. Used by permission of the publisher.]

.... I have been investigating natural rights this summer and have found that no deduction of the *reality* of the concept of right exists anywhere. All explanations of it are merely formal, semantic explanations, which already presuppose both the existence within us of such a concept (as a fact) as well as the meaning of this concept. Such explanations do not even adequately deduce this concept from the fact of the moral law (which fact I am equally unwilling to accept, unless it too is deduced). In this connection, I reread Kant's *Groundwork for the Metaphysics of Morals*, and found that *here* if anywhere the inadequacy of Kant's principles can be concretely demonstrated, as can his presupposition of higher principles—a presupposition which he himself failed to notice.

Kant asserts and proves that some particular maxim (= *A*) contradicts the predicate universally valid for all rational beings (this predicate = *B*). I reply that this may well be; but this does not interest me, for what requires me to relate *A* to *B* at all? [Suppose that] I want to retain this maxim as mine alone. If it becomes universally valid, then of course I know that my game is spoiled. But why should I adopt maxims for myself in a certain sphere only on the condition that they can be thought of as universally valid? Kant does not answer this question at all.

.....

Kant's basic principles also contain a second gross deficiency, one which springs from the first. He says that, in accordance with maxim *A*, I ought to ask around to find out whether others agree with me. How long should I continue to seek such agreement, and when should I cease to look for it? Where does the boundary lie in this case? As I have said, Kant's answer would be: "Continue to seek agreement until you have reached the boundary of all rational being." I reply "This is just what I have been trying to do. But where is [the] boundary of all rational being? The objects of my actions are, after all, always appearances in the material world. To which of these appearances should I assign the concept of rationality and to which should I not?" "You know the answer to this question all too well," Kant would have to reply. Correct as this reply is, it is nevertheless anything but a philosophical reply. I ride a horse without asking its permission and without wishing to have it ride me in turn. Why do I have more qualms when it comes to the man who lends me the horse? The fact that the poor animal cannot defend itself is quite beside the point. Thus it will always remain a very delicate question whether, though my act is supported in this case by general opinion, I am not just as unjustified in riding a horse as the Russian nobleman is when he gives away his serfs, or sells them, or beats them for the fun of it—for his act too is supported by the general opinion.

Appendix G: From Friedrich von Schiller and Wolfgang von Goethe, Xenian (1796)

[Johann Christoph Friedrich von Schiller (1759-1805) was a poet, essayist, and playwright. Outside of philosophy, Schiller is perhaps most widely known for such plays as *Don Carlos* (1787) and *Maria Stuart* (1800). However, his essays include philosophical works, such as *On Grace and Dignity* (1793), in which he criticizes the schism between reason and sentiment in Kant's moral philosophy. (Kant explicitly responds to these criticisms in a note in *Religion Within the Limits of Reason Alone*.) Schiller's most substantial philosophical work is the *Letters on Aesthetic Education* (1795), in which he draws on the work of several Enlightenment philosophers, including Kant. The following is a well-known excerpt from "The Philosophers," in *Xenian*, on which he collaborated with his friend and fellow writer Johann Wolfgang von Goethe (1749-1832).

The translation is by Allen W. Wood. Reprinted from Allen W. Wood, *Kant's Ethical Thought*, Cambridge University Press, 1999. Reprinted with the publisher's permission.]

Scruples of Conscience

I like to serve my friends, but unfortunately I do it by inclination
And so often I am bothered by the thought that I am not virtuous.

Decision

There is no other way but this! You must seek to despise them
And do with repugance what duty bids you.

Appendix H: From Georg Wilhelm Friedrich Hegel, Lectures on the History of Philosophy *(1831)*

[Georg Wilhelm Fricdrich Hegel (1770-1831) is an important philosopher both in his own right and as a critic of Kant. That Kant's work had a strong influence on Hegel's thought is apparent in both Hegel's speculative and practical philosophy. Hegel's works include *The Phenomenology of Spirit* (1807), the *Science of Logic* (1812, 1816), the *Encyclopedia of Philosophical Sciences* (1817, 1827, 1830), and the *Philosophy of Right* (1821). The following criticism of Kant's formula of universal law is excerpted from Hegel's *Lectures on the History of Philosophy*, originally published in 1831, from lecture notes taken by his students at the University of Berlin.

From *Lectures on the History of Philosophy*, translation by E.S. Haldane and Frances H. Simson, New York: Routledge & Kegan Paul/The Humanities Press (1955 [1892]), pp. 460-61 (footnotes omitted). Reprinted by permission of Thomson Publishing Services on behalf of Routledge.]

.... [The] sole form of [the categorical imperative] is nothing more or less than agreement with itself, universality; the formal principle of legislation in this internal solitude comes to no determination, or this is abstraction only. The universal, the non-contradiction of self, is without content, something which comes to be reality in the practical sphere just as little as in the theoretical. The universal moral law Kant therefore expresses thus.... "Act from maxims" (the law is also to be my particular law), "which are capable of becoming universal laws."

Thus for the determination of duty (for the question which meets us is, what is the duty for the free will) Kant has contributed nothing but the form of identity, which is the law of abstract Understanding. To defend one's fatherland, to promote the happiness of another, is a duty, not because of the content, but because it is a duty.... The content as such is indeed not what holds good universally in the moral law, because it contradicts itself. For benevolence, for instance, enjoins: "Give your possessions to the poor," but if all give away what they have, beneficence is done away with.... Even with abstract identity, however, we do not get a step further, for every content which is put into this form is by being so put freed from self-contradiction. But nothing would be lost if it were not put into this form at all. With regard to property, for instance, the law of my actions is this: Property ought to be respected, for the opposite of this cannot be universal law. That is correct, but it is quite a formal determination: If property is, then it is. Property is here presupposed, but this determination may also in the same way be omitted, and then there is no contradiction involved in theft: If there is no such thing as property, then it is not respected. This is the defect in the principle of Kant and Fichte, that it is really formal; chill duty is the final undigested lump left within the stomach, the revelation given to Reason.

Appendix I: From Henry Sidgwick, The Methods of Ethics (1907)

[Henry Sidgwick (1838-1900) is one of the most influential utilitarian moral philosophers. The following contains most of his appendix to *The Methods of Ethics*, which was first published in 1874. (This excerpt, however, is taken from the seventh edition, published by Macmillan and Company in 1907). The appendix is a revised reprint of an article that first appeared the journal *Mind* XIII (51) (1888). I have retained Sidgwick's British spelling.]

The Kantian Conception of Free Will

My aim is to show that, in different parts of Kant's exposition of his doctrine, two essentially different conceptions are expressed by the same word freedom; while yet Kant does not appear to be conscious of any variation in the meaning of the term. [In the one sense, Freedom=Rationality, so that a man is free in proportion as he acts in accordance with Reason.] I do not in the least object to this use of the term Freedom, on account of its deviation from ordinary usage. On the contrary, I think it has much support in men's natural expression of ordinary moral experience in discourse. In the conflict that is continually going on in all of us, between non-rational impulses and what we recognise as dictates of practical reason, we are in the habit of identifying ourselves with the latter rather than with the former: as Whewell says, "we speak of Desire, Love, Anger, as mastering us, and of ourselves as controlling them"—we continually call men "slaves" of appetite or passion, whereas no one was ever called a slave of reason. If, therefore, the term Freedom had not already been appropriated by moralists to another meaning—if it were merely a question of taking it from ordinary discourse and stamping it with greater precision for purposes of ethical discussion—I should make no objection to the statement that "a man is a free agent in proportion as he acts rationally." But, what English defenders of man's free agency have generally been concerned to maintain, is that "man has a freedom of *choice* between good and evil," which is realised or manifested when he deliberately chooses evil just as much as when he deliberately chooses good; and it is clear that if we say that a man is a free agent in proportion as he acts rationally, we cannot also say, in the same sense of the term, that it is by his free choice that he acts irrationally when he does so act. The notions of Freedom must be admitted to be fundamentally different in the two statements: and though usage might fairly allow the word Freedom to represent either notion, if only one or the other of the above-mentioned propositions were affirmed, to use it to represent both, in affirming both propositions, is obviously inconvenient; and it implies a confusion of thought so to use it, without pointing out the difference of meaning.

If this be admitted, the next thing is to show that Kant does use the term in this double way. In arguing this, it will be convenient to have names for what we admit to be two distinct ideas. Accordingly, the kind of freedom which I first mentioned—which a man is said to manifest more in proportion as he acts more under the guidance of reason—shall be referred to as 'Good' or 'Rational Freedom,' and the freedom that is manifested in choosing between good and evil shall be called 'Neutral' or 'Moral Freedom.'[1]

.... It will be easily understood that, as he does not himself distinguish the two conceptions, it is naturally impossible for the most careful reader always to tell which is to be understood; but there are many passages where his argument unmistakably requires the one, and many other passages where it unmistakably requires the other. Speaking broadly, I may say that, wherever Kant has to connect the notion of Freedom with that of Moral Responsibility or moral imputation, he, like all other moralists who have maintained Free Will in this connexion, means (chiefly, but not solely) Neutral Freedom—Freedom exhibited in choosing wrong as much as in choosing right. Indeed, in such passages it is with the Freedom of the wrong-chooser that he is primarily concerned: since it is the wrong-chooser that he especially wishes to prevent from shifting his responsibility on to causes beyond his control. On the other hand, when what he has to prove is the possibility of disinterested obedience to Law as such, without the intervention of sensible impulses, when he seeks to exhibit the independence of Reason in influencing choice, then in many

---

1   The terms 'rational' and 'moral' seem to me most appropriate when I wish to suggest the affinity between the two notions: the terms 'good' and 'neutral' seem preferable when I wish to lay stress on the difference. [H.S.]

though not all his statements he explicitly identifies Freedom with this independence of Reason, and thus clearly implies the proposition that a man is free in proportion as he acts rationally. As an example of the first kind, I will take the passage towards the close of chap. iii. of the "Analytic of Practical Reason,"[1] where he treats, in its bearing on Moral Responsibility, his peculiar metaphysical doctrine of a double kind of causation in human actions. According to Kant, every such action, regarded as a phenomenon determined in time, must be thought as a necessary result of determining causes in antecedent time—otherwise its existence would be inconceivable—but it may be also regarded in relation to the agent considered as a thing-in-himself, as the "noümenon" of which the action is a phenomenon: and the conception of Freedom may be applied to the agent so considered in relation to his phenomena. For since his existence as a noümenon is not subject to time-conditions, nothing in this noümenal existence comes under the principle of determination by antecedent causes: hence, as Kant says, "in this his existence nothing is antecedent to the determination of his will, but every action ... even the whole series of his existence as a sensible being, is in the consciousness of his supersensible existence nothing but the result of his causality as noümenon." This is the well-known metaphysical solution of the difficulty of reconciling Free Will with the Universality of physical causation: I am not now concerned to criticise it, my point is that if we accept this view of Freedom at all, it must obviously be Neutral Freedom: it must express the relation of a noümenon that manifests itself as a scoundrel to a series of bad volitions, in which the moral law is violated, no less than the relation of a noümenon that manifests itself as a saint to good or rational volitions, in which the moral law or categorical imperative is obeyed. And, as I before said, Kant in this passage—being especially concerned to explain the possibility of moral imputation, and justify the judicial sentences of conscience—especially takes as his illustrations noümena that exhibit bad phenomena. The question he expressly raises is "How a man who commits a theft" can "be called quite free" at the moment of committing it? and answers that it is in virtue of his "transcendental freedom" that "the rational being can justly say

---

1 *Werke*, v. 100-104 (Hartenstein). [H.S.] Part of Kant's *Critique of Practical Reason*, see especially 5:95-100 of the Prussian Academy edition; all additional page numbers provided below by me refer to that edition.

of *every unlawful action* that he performs that he could very well have left it undone," although as phenomenon it is determined by antecedents, and so necessary; "for it, with all the past which determines it, belongs to the one single phenomenon of his character which he makes for himself, in consequence of which he imputes to himself" the bad actions that result necessarily from his bad character taken in conjunction with other causes. Hence, however he may account for his error from bad habits which he has allowed to grow on him, whatever art he may use to paint to himself an unlawful act he remembers as something in which he was carried away by the stream of physical necessity, this cannot protect him from self-reproach:—not even if he have shown depravity so early that he may reasonably be thought to have been born in a morally hopeless condition—he will still be rightly judged, and will judge himself "just as responsible as any other man": since in relation to his noümenal self his life as a whole, from first to last, is to be regarded as a single phenomenon resulting from an absolutely free choice.

I need not labour this point further; it is evident that the necessities of Kant's metaphysical explanation of moral responsibility make him express with peculiar emphasis and fulness the notion of what I have called Neutral Freedom, a kind of causality manifested in bad and irrational volitions no less than in the good and rational.

On the other hand, it is no less easy to find passages in which the term Freedom seems to me most distinctly to stand for Good or Rational Freedom. Indeed, such passages are, I think, more frequent than those in which the other meaning is primarily required. Thus he tells us that "a free will must find its principle of determination in the [moral] 'Law,'"[1] and that "freedom, whose causality can be determined only by the law, consists in just this, that it restricts all inclinations by the condition of obedience to pure law."[2] Whereas, in the argument previously examined, his whole effort was to prove that the noümenon or supersensible being, of which each volition is a phenomenon, exercises "free causality" in unlawful acts, he tells us elsewhere, in the same treatise, that the "supersensible nature" of rational beings, who have also a "sensible nature," is their "existence according to laws which are independent of every empirical condition, and therefore belong to the autonomy of pure [practical] reason."[3] Similarly, in an earlier work,

---

1 *Werke*, v. 30. [H.S.] *Critique of Practical Reason*, 5:29.
2 *Ibid.*, 83. [H.S.] *Critique of Practical Reason*, 5:78.
3 *Ibid.*, 46. [H.S.] *Critique of Practical Reason*, 5:43.

he explains that "since the conception of causality involves that of laws ... though freedom is not a property of the will depending on physical laws, yet it is not for that reason lawless; on the contrary, it must be a causality according to immutable laws, but of a peculiar kind; otherwise, a free will would be a chimæra (*Unding*)."[1] And this immutable law of the "free" or "autonomous" will is, as he goes on to say, the fundamental principle of morality, "so that a free will and a will subject to moral laws are one and the same."

I have quoted this last phrase, not because it clearly exhibits the notion of Rational Freedom,—on the contrary, it rather shows how easily this notion may be confounded with the other. A will subject to its own moral laws *may* mean a will that, so far as free, conforms to these laws; but it also *may* be conceived as capable of freely disobeying these laws—exercising Neutral Freedom. But when Freedom is said to be a "causality according to immutable laws" the ambiguity is dispelled; for this evidently cannot mean merely a faculty of laying down laws which may or may not be obeyed; it must mean that the will, *quâ* free, acts in accordance with these laws;—the human being, doubtless, often acts contrary to them; but then, according to this view, its choice in such actions is determined not "freely" but "mechanically," by "physical" and "empirical" springs of action.

If any further argument is necessary to show that Kantian "Freedom" must sometimes be understood as Rational or Good Freedom, I may quote one or two of the numerous passages in which Kant, either expressly or by implication, identifies Will and Reason; for this identification obviously excludes the possibility of Will's choosing between Reason and non-rational impulses. Thus in the *Grundlegung zur Metaphysik der Sitten*,[2] he tells us that "as Reason is required to deduce actions from laws, Will is nothing but pure practical reason"; and, similarly, in the *Kritik der praktischen Vernunft*, he speaks of the "objective reality of a pure Will or, *which is the same thing*, a pure practical reason."[3]

---

1 *Werke*, iv, 294. [H.S.] *Groundwork*, 4:446-47.
2 *Werke*, iv, 260 (Hartenstein). [H.S.] *Groundwork*, 4:412.
3 *Werke*, v, 58. See an acute discussion of Kant's perplexing use of the term "Will" in Prof. Schurman's *Kantian Ethics*, which has anticipated me in the above quotations. [H.S.] *Critique of Practical Reason*, 5:55. The *Wille/Willkür* distinction referred to in Appendix D, p. 150, n. 1 may be relevant to understanding some of Kant's claims about freedom of the will. See Henry E. Allison, *Kant's Theory of Freedom* (Cambridge: Cambridge UP, 1990), 129-36; and Lewis White Beck, *A Commentary on Kant's Critique of Practical Reason* (Chicago: U of Chicago P, 1960), 176-208.

Accordingly, whereas in some passages[1] the "autonomy" which he identifies with "Freedom" is spoken of as "autonomy of *will*," in others we are told that the "moral law expresses nothing else than autonomy of the pure practical *reason*: that is, Freedom."[2]

I think that I have now established the verbal ambiguity that I undertook to bring home to Kant's account of Free Will; I have shown that in his exposition this fundamental term oscillates between incompatible meanings. But it may, perhaps, be thought that the defect thus pointed out can be cured by a merely verbal correction: that the substance of Kant's ethical doctrine may still be maintained, and may still be connected with his metaphysical doctrine. It may still be held that Reason dictates that we should at all times act from a maxim that we can will to be a universal law, and that we should do this from pure regard for reason and reason's law, admitting that it is a law which we are free to disobey; and it may still be held that the reality of this moral freedom is to be reconciled with the universality of physical causation by conceiving it as a relation between the agent's noümenal self—independent of time-conditions—and his character as manifested in time; the only correction required being to avoid identifying Freedom and Goodness or Rationality as attributes of agents or actions.

I should quite admit that the most important parts both of Kant's doctrine of morality, and of his doctrine of Freedom may be saved:—or I should perhaps rather say that the latter may be left to conduct an unequal struggle with the modern notions of heredity and evolution: at any rate I admit that it is not fundamentally affected by my present argument. But I think that a good deal more will have to go from a corrected edition of Kantism than merely the "word" Freedom in certain passages, if the confusion introduced by the ambiguity of this word is to be eliminated in the manner that I have suggested. I think that the whole topic of the "heteronomy" of the will, when it yields to empirical or sensible impulses, will have to be abandoned or profoundly modified. And I am afraid that most readers of Kant will feel the loss to be serious; since nothing in Kant's ethical writing is more fascinating than the idea—which he expresses repeatedly in various forms—that a man realises the aim of his true self when he obeys the moral law, whereas, when he wrongly allows his action

---

1   E.g. *Werke*, iv, 296. [H.S.] *Groundwork*, 4:449.
2   E.g. *Werke*, v, 35. [H.S.] *Critique of Practical Reason*, 5:33.

to be determined by empirical or sensible stimuli, he becomes subject to physical causation, to laws of a brute outer world. But if we dismiss the identification of Freedom and Rationality, and accept definitely and singly Kant's other notion of Freedom as expressing the relation of the human thing-in-itself to its phenomenon, I am afraid that this spirit-stirring appeal to the sentiment of Liberty must be dismissed as idle rhetoric. For the life of the saint must be as much subject—in any particular portion of it—to the necessary laws of physical causation as the life of the scoundrel: and the scoundrel must exhibit and express his characteristic self-hood in his transcendental choice of a bad life, as much as the saint does in his transcendental choice of a good one. If, on the other hand, to avoid this result, we take the other horn of the dilemma, and identify inner freedom with rationality, then a more serious excision will be required. For, along with 'Neutral' or 'Moral' Freedom, the whole Kantian view of the relation of the noümenon to the empirical character will have to be dropped, and with it must go the whole Kantian method of maintaining moral responsibility and moral imputation: in fact, all that has made Kant's doctrine interesting and impressive to English advocates of Free Will (in the ordinary sense), even when they have not been convinced of its soundness.

Suggested Reading

[This list provides suggestions for further reading for those interested in Kant, his ethics, and his philosophy more generally. Given the vast number of works on Kant, I could not even come close to including everything worth reading. Nearly all of the entries here are books. Many of these books are collections, containing many relevant articles or chapters by one or more authors; I have not listed these articles or chapters separately.]

1. Kant's Works

Some of Kant's best-known works—besides *Groundwork*—are *Critique of Pure Reason*, *Critique of Practical Reason*, and *Critique of the Power of Judgment*. *Prolegomena to Any Future Metaphysics* is a short, though challenging, introduction to Kant's metaphysics and epistemology. The *Metaphysics of Morals* is Kant's most complete work of normative ethics. Readers are encouraged to see the Introduction, Brief Chronology, and Appendices B–E of the present edition for ideas about which of Kant's other works may be of interest. One can find Kant's works in many editions, of which *Gesammelte Schriften* edited by the Prussian Academy (Berlin: Walter de Gruyter, 1902) is the standard in Kant's original German. Some of the newest and best translations of Kant's works are found in the Cambridge Editions of the Works of Immanuel Kant, Paul Guyer and Allen Wood, series editors. Among the editions already published in this series are the following:

Gregor, Mary J., ed. and trans. *Practical Philosophy*. Cambridge: Cambridge UP, 1996.
Guyer, Paul, and Wood, Allen W., ed. and trans. *Critique of Pure Reason*. Cambridge: Cambridge UP, 1998.
—. *Critique of the Power of Judgment*. Cambridge: Cambridge UP, 2000.
Guyer, Paul, ed. Bowman, Curtis, Guyer, Paul, and Rauscher, Frederick, trans. *Notes and Fragments*. Cambridge: Cambridge UP, 2005.
Heath, Peter and Schneewind, J.B. ed. Heath, Peter trans. *Lectures on Ethics*. Cambridge: Cambridge UP, 1997.
Wood, Allen W. and di Giovanni, George, ed. and trans. *Religion and Rational Theology*. Cambridge: Cambridge UP 1996.

The series will also include Kant's works on anthropology, history, education, and natural science.

2. Correspondence

Zweig, Arnulf, ed. and trans. *Correspondence*. Cambridge: Cambridge UP, 1999.

3. Biography

Cassier, Ernst. *Kant's Life and Thought*. Translated by James Haden, introduction by Stephan Körner. New Haven: Yale UP, 1981.

Kuehn, Manfred. *Kant: A Biography*. Cambridge: Cambridge UP, 2001.

4. Introduction to Kant's Ethics

Acton, H.B. *Kant's Moral Philosophy*. London: Macmillan, 1970.

O'Neill, Onora. "The Moral Perplexities of Famine and World Hunger." *Matters of Life and Death*. Ed. Tom Regan. New York: Random House, 1980.

Sullivan, Roger. *An Introduction to Kant's Ethics*. Cambridge: Cambridge UP, 1994.

Walker, Ralph. *Kant and the Moral Law*. New York: Routledge, 1999.

5. Kant's *Groundwork for the Metaphysics of Morals*

Guyer, Paul, ed. *Kant's Groundwork for the Metaphysics of Morals: Critical Essays*. Lanham, Maryland: Rowman and Littlefield, 1998.

Wood, Allen W., ed. and trans. *Groundwork for the Metaphysics of Morals*. New Haven: Yale UP, 2002. (This is a new translation with many helpful notes and critical essays by the editor and three other moral philosophers.)

6. Kant's *Critique of Practical Reason*
Beck, Lewis White. *A Commentary on Kant's Critique of Practical Reason*. Chicago: U of Chicago P, 1960.

7. Kant's *Metaphysics of Morals*

Gregor, Mary J. *Laws of Freedom: A Study of Kant's Method of Applying the Categorical Imperative in the* Metaphysik der Sitten. Oxford: Basil Blackwell, 1963.

Timmons, Mark, ed. *Kant's Metaphysics of Morals*. Oxford: Oxford UP, 2002.

8. Kant's Ethical Theory

Allison, Henry E. *Kant's Theory of Freedom*. Cambridge: Cambridge UP, 1990.

Baron, Marcia W. *Kantian Ethics Almost Without Apology*. Ithaca, NY: Cornell UP, 1995.

Denis, Lara. *Moral Self-Regard: Duties to Oneself in Kant's Moral Theory*. New York and London: Garland, 2001.

Guyer, Paul. *Kant and the Experience of Freedom*. Cambridge: Cambridge UP, 1993.

—. *Kant on Freedom, Law, and Happiness*. Cambridge: Cambridge UP, 2000.

Herman, Barbara. *The Practice of Moral Judgment*. Cambridge, MA: Harvard UP, 1993.

Hill, Thomas E., Jr. *Autonomy and Self-Respect*. Cambridge: Cambridge UP, 1991.

—. *Dignity and Practical Reason*. Ithaca, NY: Cornell UP, 1992

Korsgaard, Christine M. *Creating the Kingdom of Ends*. New York: Cambridge UP, 1996.

Kerstein, Samuel J. *Kant's Search for the Supreme Principle of Morality*. Cambridge: Cambridge UP, 2002.

Nell, Onora (O'Neill). *Acting on Principle: An Essay in Kantian Ethics*. New York: Columbia UP, 1975.

O'Neill, Onora. *Constructions of Reason*. Cambridge: Cambridge UP, 1989.

Wood, Allen W. *Kant's Ethical Thought*. Cambridge: Cambridge UP, 1999.

9. Kant's Political Theory

Murphy, Jeffrie. *Kant: The Philosophy of Right*. London: Macmillan, 1970.

Rosen, Allen D. *Kant's Theory of Justice*. Ithaca, NY: Cornell UP, 1993.

Williams, Howard. *Kant's Political Philosophy*. New York: St. Martin's Press, 1983.

10. Kant's Aesthetics

Allison, Henry E. *Kant's Theory of Taste*. Cambridge: Cambridge UP, 2001.
Guyer, Paul. *Kant and the Claims of Taste*. Cambridge, MA: Harvard UP, 1979.

11. Kant's Anthropology and Philosophy of History

Anderson-Gold, Sharon. *Unnecessary Evil: History and Moral Progress in the Philosophy of Immanuel Kant*. Albany: State University of New York Press, 2001.
Jacobs, Brian, and Patrick Kain, eds. *Essays on Kant's Anthropology*. Cambridge: Cambridge UP, 2003.
Louden, Robert B. *Kant's Impure Ethics: From Rational Beings to Human Beings*. New York: Oxford UP, 2000.
Yovel, Yirmiahu. *Kant and the Philosophy of History*. Princeton: Princeton UP, 1981.

12. Kant's Philosophy of Religion

Hare, John E. *The Moral Gap: Kantian Ethics, Human Limits and God's Assistance*. Oxford: Clarendon, 1996.
Wood, Allen W. *Kant's Moral Religion*. Ithaca, NY: Cornell UP, 1970.
Wood, Allen W. *Kant's Rational Theology*. Ithaca, NY: Cornell UP, 1978.

13. Kant's Theoretical Philosophy

Allison, Henry E. *Kant's Transcendental Idealism: An Interpretation and Defense*. New Haven: Yale UP, 1983.
Guyer, Paul. *Kant and the Claims of Knowledge*. Cambridge: Cambridge UP, 1987.

14. The Historical and Philosophical Context for Kant's Philosophy

Beck, Lewis White. *Early German Philosophy: Kant and His Prede-*

cessors. Cambridge, MA: Belknap Press of Harvard University, 1969.

Beiser, Frederick. *The Fate of Reason: German Philosophy from Kant to Fichte*. Cambridge, MA: Harvard UP, 1987.

Schneewind, Jerome B. *The Invention of Autonomy*. Cambridge: Cambridge UP, 1998.

—. *Moral Philosophy from Montaigne to Kant*. Volumes I and II. Cambridge: Cambridge UP, 1990.

15. Other Anthologies

Guyer, Paul, ed. *The Cambridge Companion to Kant*. Cambridge: Cambridge UP, 1992.

—. *The Cambridge Companion to Kant–Second Edition*. Cambridge: Cambridge UP, forthcoming.

Kneller, Jane and Sidney Axinn, eds. *Autonomy and Community: Readings in Contemporary Kantian Social Philosophy*. Albany: State University of New York Press, 1998.

Schott, Robin May, ed. *Feminist Interpretations of Immanuel Kant*. University Park, PA: Pennsylvania State UP, 1997.

Index

free will, 33, 92, 106, 111–12, 115–16, 130, 182–83, 186. *See also* autonomy of the will; formula of autonomy
    Sidgwick's criticism, 181
freedom, 35, 106, 110, 114–15, 117, 124, 150, 156, 159, 181
    assumption of, 34
    and causality of one's own will, 108
    'Good' or 'Rational Freedom,' 182, 184
    idea of, 116
    and law of nature, 112
    and natural necessity, 111
    as negative characteristic, 113
    neutral, 182–85, 187
    positive conception of, 103
    presupposed as property of all rational beings, 104–5
    public use of reason, 120–21
    "transcendental freedom," 183
FUL. *See* formula of universal law
FULN. *See* formula of the universal law of nature
Fundamental Principles of the Metaphysic of Morals (Kant), 45

Garve, Christian, 14, 70n1, 141–42, 144–47
general division of rights, 156
generality, 84
gifts of fortune, 55
Giovanni, George di, 149
given ends, 79
God, 40, 69, 127, 136–39, 144
Goethe, Johann Wolfgang von, 177
good in itself, 74
good will, 17–20, 27, 55, 58, 110
    absolutely good will, 85, 95, 101, 103
    as good itself, 56
gratitude, 173n1
Greek philosophy, 49, 128, 138
Gregor, Mary J., *Kant: Practical Philosophy*, 141, 153
Groundwork for the Metaphysics of Morals (Kant), 11–14, 17, 36, 38–39, 45, 53, 175
    purpose of, 16
Grundlegung zur Metaphysik der Sitten (Kant), 45, 185

Haldane, E.S., *Lectures on the History of Philosophy*, 179

happiness, 18, 21–22, 40, 55–58, 60–61, 66, 75, 77–78, 89, 99,
    100n1, 127–29, 131–32, 136, 138, 144
  of others, 164–65
  private, 99
  worthiness for, 139, 142, 144, 148
Hegel, Georg Wilhelm Friedrich, 11
  Lectures on the History of Philosophy, 12, 179
Herder, Johann Gottfried, 14
heteronomy, 91, 99, 108
  of nature, 109
  of the will, 30, 98, 101, 186
highest good, 40, 127–32, 134–35, 137, 139, 142, 143n1
holiness, 135
holy wills, 21, 74, 97
human agency. *See* rational agents
human beings, 36
  as one category of rational beings, 17, 72
human nature, 85
  common, 65–66, 69, 72
  frailty and impurity, 67
  particular constitution of, 84, 99
human reason, 72, 85
humanity, 26
  as an end in itself, 36, 89
Hume, David, 14
Hutcheson, Francis, 14, 100n1
hypothesis, 138
hypothetical imperatives, 21, 74–76, 80, 86, 98

idea of moral perfection, 69
ideal conceptions, 73
"ideas," 108
imagination, 78
imitation, 69
immaturity, 119–20, 124–25
immortality of the soul, 127, 135–36, 144
  as a postulate of pure practical reason, 134
imperative, 21–22, 73–75. *See also* categorical imperative
  analytic, 79
  conditional, 101
  of duty, 81
  hypothetical, 21, 74–76, 80, 86, 98
  moral, 77, 79, 118, 157

misology, 57
Mohammed's paradise, 133
moral concepts
    a priori in reason, 72
moral feeling, 99–100, 115
moral final end, 143n1
moral health, 167
moral imperatives, 77, 157
    incomprehensibility, 157
moral judgment, 95, 115
moral law(s), 23n1, 33–35, 39, 51–52, 71, 106, 134, 142, 150.
    See also law of freedom
    holding good for every rational being, 72
moral necessitation. *See* necessitation
moral philosophy, 49, 51–52
moral prosperity, 167
moral requirements, 27
moral value, 20
moral well-being, 165
moral worth, 18–20, 59–62, 67–68, 97. *See also* absolute
    worth
    deficiency in, 161
morality, 50, 76, 92–93, 97, 102, 105, 109, 116, 128, 136
    as autonomously legislated, 30
    and capacity to make choices, 28
    cultivation of, 163
    principle of, 91
    supreme good, 132
morally good disposition, 94
motivation, 52, 58n1, 86
murdering oneself, 168. *See also* suicide example

narrow duty, 161
narrow obligation, 162
natural dialectic, 66
natural ends, 24
natural philosophy, 49
natural rights, 156, 175
natural welfare, 164
nature, 57, 81, 111
    system of, 90
necessary duties, 88
necessitation, 73–74, 76–77, 97, 157–58

necessity
  natural, 103, 111
  unconditional and objective, 76
need, 74n1
negative conception of freedom, 33, 103
negative duty, 165
'Neutral' or 'Moral Freedom,' 182–85, 187
Newton, Isaac, 13
normative ethics, 20, 36–37, 40
noümenon, 131, 183–84, 187
Nozick, Robert, 11

objective ends, 87
objective principle, 80n3
obligation, 51–52, 85, 97. *See also* duties
  narrow, 162
obstacles, 158
On Grace and Dignity (Schiller), 177
"On the Common Saying: 'This May Be True in Theory, but it
  Does Not Apply in Practice,'" 12, 141
opposition (*antagonismus*) of inclination, 84
ought, 73–74, 105, 110–11, 115
  unconditional, 158

pathological interest, 74n1
perfect and imperfect duties, 24, 81, 168
perfection, 99
  natural, 163
  ontological conception, 100
  perfecting of oneself, 167
  principle of, 101
  theological conception of, 100
perfectionism, 14
persons, 87, 96
"Philosophers, The" (Schiller), 177
physical causation, 186–87
physics, 49–50
  as philosophy of nature, 86
plurality of the matter, 95
political writings, 30
popular philosophy, 70–72
positive conception of freedom, 103–4
positive (statutory) right, 156

From the Publisher

A name never says it all, but the word "Broadview" expresses a good deal of the philosophy behind our company. We are open to a broad range of academic approaches and political viewpoints. We pay attention to the broad impact book publishing and book printing has in the wider world; for some years now we have used 100% recycled paper for most titles. Our publishing program is internationally oriented and broad-ranging. Our individual titles often appeal to a broad readership too; many are of interest as much to general readers as to academics and students.

Founded in 1985, Broadview remains a fully independent company owned by its shareholders—not an imprint or subsidiary of a larger multinational.

For the most accurate information on our books (including information on pricing, editions, and formats) please visit our website at www.broadviewpress.com. Our print books and ebooks are also available for sale on our site.

broadview press
www.broadviewpress.com